ALVIN SANDERS

REDEMPTIVE POVERTY WORK

EXPANDED EDITION

Practical Steps for Faith Leaders Serving People Experiencing Poverty

Requests for information should be sent to World Impact.

Visit www.worldimpact.org for contact information.

Cover design: Bryana Anderle (YouPublish.com)
Interior design: Sara Hook (YouPublish.com)
Editorial and art direction: Chad Harrington (YouPublish.com)

To all those who work tirelessly to make the world a better place for those living in poverty. May you not grow weary in doing good.

Contents

Introduction

THIS BOOK IS FOR MANY people, but it stands out in its own unique way. There is no shortage of books that help people understand poverty or describe the struggles of those living in it. However, few books are aimed explicitly at faith-based organizational leaders and individuals committed to working with people experiencing poverty. I believe there is a large community of dedicated poverty workers worldwide—people on a mission to make a difference for those in need. You are:

- Pastors striving toward community transformation.
- Faith-based nonprofit leaders changing lives.
- People in "helping professions" (nurses, doctors, therapists, teachers, social workers, etc.) who work specifically to make a difference in society.
- Business owners who are working not only toward a financial bottom line but also pursuing a moral and social one.
- Volunteers who may not feel a vocational call toward those experiencing poverty, but who faithfully contribute their time, talent, and treasure to the cause.

Regardless of why you picked up this book, you probably want to follow in the footsteps of Christ—and change lives and neighborhoods along the way. Redemptive poverty work is about being with God as you do what you have been called to do, not just reading about it. So, if you share my "get-to-the-point" mindset because you are ready to get back to work, this is the right book for you! I have made it very practical. My goal is to invest in a community of highly influential individuals known as *redemptive poverty workers.*

Redemptive poverty work has a vision that goes beyond merely solving problems. It aims to transform lives, neighborhoods, and systems—without compromising anyone's integrity or relationships. Redemptive poverty work connects our story with God's larger story of renewal. It understands that poverty is not just a condition to be fixed but a brokenness to be healed, and only the power of Christ can fully restore what has been lost.

I will discuss this in more detail in Chapter 4. For now, I will share the qualities we have in common, which include loving Jesus Christ, feeling called to serve, and being gritty and faithful in our work with the poor. However, many of us are tired and heartbroken because working with people in poverty often brings disappointment. We hold high hopes and good intentions, but anyone who has done this kind of work for a while knows that hopes and intentions alone are not enough.

For many of us, serving those who are less fortunate runs deep in our bones. We could not stop serving even if we wanted to. We have made sacrifices to answer the call to serve and have poured ourselves out day after day. While we hope for acknowledgment, we are often not appreciated as we should be.

Sometimes it feels like we are fulfilling the call to serve against our will. Many of us operate in a state of exhaustion, constantly on the brink of burnout. For some, the work might be impressive, but their family is falling apart, they have no friends because they are workaholics on a mission to save the world, and they have not felt God's presence in years. For others, that ambition and drive to change the world has long since faded, leaving them to wonder if the sacrifice was truly worth it.

I have observed these things from the many redemptive poverty workers I have met over the years. Often, our biggest problem is workaholism, which can lead to burnout. I understand such circumstances personally. In the past, I thought it was part of the process, simply unavoidable. Now, I see it as a symptom of not intentionally recognizing the toll the work takes on me. Only when we identify the problem can we begin taking steps toward a solution.

So, the question is: Is workaholism sustainable? I know it is not, and you probably do too. As I enter my thirty-second year of ministry, I look around and see only a third of those I started with still showing up to do the hard work of serving those in poverty. Let me tell you, there is no substitute for establishing a strong foundation for the work God has called you to do. The harsh truth is that if you do not establish a solid foundation, it will only be a matter of when, not if, you burn out. Motivation to help people or a vision to change the world will not be enough to sustain you. I know this all too well from experience.

My Story

Before I proceed, I believe it is essential for you to understand my personal calling. 1 Peter 4:10 does a great job of defining a call: "Each of you should use whatever gift you have received to serve others, as faithful stewards of God's grace in its various forms." To me, this verse highlights the importance of each of us using our gifts and talents to help make the world a better place, which I call seeking the common good.

I believe calling is a suitable match between a person and a situation. For example, as president and CEO of World Impact, I want the staff members and the organization to leverage a person's strengths and motivation to fulfill their job responsibilities. When people use their talents and gifts effectively, it benefits both them and the organization.

Regarding my call, two gifts from my upbringing have had a profound influence on me. The first is that I had a very diverse, multiethnic childhood. Because my father was in the military, I had the unique privilege of growing up from Maine to Japan. This gift gave me an innate understanding of how to handle different cultural situations. The second came from my mother. She introduced me to the gift of experiencing the local church. Wherever we lived, Mom found a church home for us.

People ask me when I was saved, and I jokingly say I do not know! That is 100 percent because of my mom. There has never been a time in my life when I was an atheist or agnostic, and the older I get, the more I realize how much of a gift it is never to doubt God's existence. However, there was a brief period when I did not fully appreciate my relationship with Christ.

It was my first semester at a state university. For the first time in my life, church was optional, and I took full advantage of not attending—until I met a fellow student whose faith was burning brightly. He rekindled my interest in taking my faith seriously and motivated me to join the leadership team of his campus Bible study. He had a unique vision.

He believed that traditional campus ministries were not effectively reaching African American students, so his goal was for our Bible study to do so. We achieved success, as shown by our evangelism efforts, the large turnout at our midweek Bible study, and the Sunday worship services we led. In hindsight, we were essentially church planters, even if we did not realize it at the time.

Our success led to another campus ministry group inviting us to attend a conference for African American Christian college students. During Christmas break, these students gathered for a week of worship, learning, and service. This became a pivotal moment in my life. The speakers moved me during each session, but it was not just that—it was the outreach project we completed together.

We left the conference venue and boarded a bus, where my group's assignment was to visit a community facing poverty and deliver a box of groceries to a family in need. We started at a small local church, where the pastor thanked us and gave background on the neighborhood, and we learned about the people we would be visiting. Then I paired up with someone, and we received an address. Upon arrival, our goal was to build a relationship and share the gospel.

It was immediately clear that the woman we were visiting already knew the Lord, so no introduction was needed. We discussed her needs and asked for her prayer requests. She mentioned she had not seen her son in months because of his drug addiction, so we prayed for him. I experienced a "Book of Acts" moment (meaning it felt supernatural) when I opened my eyes.

Her son was sitting at the kitchen counter, eating some of the groceries we had brought. I had not heard him come in, and based on everyone's expressions, neither had they. We left the awkward scene so that mother and son could reunite. Despite the discomfort, I was on fire—I had just seen the Lord move! The entire group gathered again at the church, and my ministry partner and I shared our experiences.

Then the great experience turned into a terrible one. As the bus was leaving to take our group back to the conference venue, I saw the young man who had only just miraculously appeared at his mother's apartment, on a street corner buying drugs. I guessed that he had gathered some food and money from his mom and headed back to the streets. I wanted to jump off the bus and stop him, but that did not happen.

Instead, I returned home a changed person. I honestly was not the same as when I walked back onto campus. During that trip, my life's calling was awakened. I wanted to be there for that mother and son, and I realized I could do so if I changed my vocational pursuit. By the fall, I had transferred from a state university to a Bible college and began to fulfill my calling.

At this point in my life, I divide my calling into two eras: before and after burnout. The experience of doing ministry before burnout can be described as gritty, faithful, and tiring—yet productive. During that time, my most significant accomplishments include planting an urban church and establishing a Christian Community

Development Corporation (CCDC) in a neighborhood that was then the second most violent in the U.S., all while earning a bachelor's and two graduate degrees. Sounds great, right? However, something felt wrong.

One of my saddest memories from that time was being home one night and having dinner with my family. My youngest daughter, who was a toddler at the time, looked at me and asked, "Daddy, why are you home?" I will never forget the look of confusion on her little face. She was clueless about why I was there. I recall having a long conversation with my wife that night about the changes I could make to be more present for them. Still, I did not change much.

The turning point happened when I shifted from pastoring and leading the CCDC to working for my denomination. For several months, people would see me and comment on how much better I looked. Did I lose weight? Get new glasses? Go on vacation? These were people who had known me for years and noticed that something about me was very different.

It took me a while to figure it out. When I shifted to working for the denomination, they taught me how to pace myself. Looking back, I believe that during my last year as a pastor, I was burned out. I was still productive, but I was running on fumes. It had become such a way of life that I knew no other way. I thought I was only doing what was necessary because of my call. Now I realize differently. I wish I had known then what I know now—that you can work effectively with those experiencing poverty in a sustainable way.

Burnout Is Optional

My hope is for you to fulfill your calling without burning out because you do not have to. This book serves as a repository for what I have learned during the post-burnout phase of my life. My insights come from the toughest school in the world—Hard Knocks. Everything you will read is a mix of distilled wisdom from my mistakes and principles I have learned and now practice every day.

Figure 1: Our Firm Foundation

I have arranged these principles like a three-legged stool; the content is divided into three sections. Think of each section as a stool leg—a solid foundation you can rely on to support you in your work. A strong understanding of these concepts will enable you to serve as co-laborers with Christ, rather than burned-out heroes. I use fictional stories to illustrate the types of people in the redemptive poverty work community and to reinforce the principle being discussed in each chapter. I will often ask you to imagine yourself in a specific scenario.

The first three chapters (stool leg one) focus on *spiritual formation*. We must avoid the trap of turning our work into our worship; instead, we should develop healthy spiritual rhythms and find peers to help refine our talents and gifts. Think of practicing these as a way to build "muscle memory" for our calling.

However, we need to combine our spiritual formation with two other important foundational pieces. Chapters four through six (stool leg two) focus on engaging the primary *stressors we face.* They explain the weights that can break us, such as maintaining the proper mindset, posture, and pace. Finally, chapters seven through nine (stool leg three) cover the essential *skillsets we need*, including community care, emotional intelligence, and faithful leadership.

Let us rise to the occasion. Let us be the answer to someone's silent prayer. Let us live out the gospel through our actions, our buildings, our budgets, and our hearts. The world is watching! More importantly, God is calling. Let us respond with courage, creativity, and compassion. Let us measure our impact by the presence of peace in our neighborhoods, the reduction of suffering in our world, and the stories of restoration that unfold. May the testimonies of those we serve be the primary measure of our success.

We know the work will stretch us. It will challenge our assumptions. It will cost us comfort and require humility. Yet, the reward will be transformed lives, revitalized neighborhoods, and the witness of a living faith shining like a city on a hill. This is the kind of Christianity our world needs—not one hidden behind stained glass but one walking boldly in the streets.

It is time to dream. Envision the organizations we serve as launchpads for healing, reconciliation, and creativity. This will require training and teaching people, empowering them to collaborate, innovate, and take Spirit-guided risks. We cannot do this alone, and we were never meant to. God calls us into communities not just to serve others but so we might be transformed ourselves.

The people we walk with shape us just as much as we shape them. That is the beauty of redemptive presence: mutual blessing and growth. Let us be a beacon of hope, a stronghold of justice, and a refuge of belonging. Let our lives be open to the lonely, the curious, the hurting, and the eager. May our work reflect the ministry of Jesus, who moved with compassion, spoke truth to power, and laid down His life to uplift others.

The work ahead is not easy, but it is sacred and worth every bit of effort we put into it. Because at the core of this mission is love. Not sentimentality, but the tough, persistent, sacrificial love that changes things. Let us hold fast to that love. Let it guide our strategies and our service. Let it inspire our imagination for what the church can become. Additionally, when the journey gets tough, may we remember the One who walks beside us, who said in Matthew 25:40, "Truly I tell you, whatever you did for one of the least of these brothers and sisters of mine, you did for me."

STOOL LEG ONE: Spiritual Formation

SPIRITUAL FORMATION IS THE GRADUAL transformation of a person into the likeness of Christ. It is less a project to control and more a reality to live in, like a house. Over time, desires shift, reflexes soften, and hope becomes a steady habit of the heart. The change is often subtle.

It unfolds in ordinary places. A work commute may turn into a worship service, or hanging out at a friend's place may become a prayer gathering. The quiet before a meeting, the ache after conflict, the joy of sharing a meal—each moment becomes part of the clay the Spirit molds. Formation flows through Scripture and worship, as well as through silence, fatigue, and surprise. Nothing is wasted; everything is significant.

Community shapes the process. In healthy relationships, truth finds a place to land and grace has space to move. Confession does not humiliate but humanizes. Celebration is not performance; it is witnessing. Elders and children alike become signs of God's patience. We learn that holiness is not distance from people, but a deeper presence with them.

There are seasons. Some feel like spring—freshness, clarity, new beginnings. Others resemble winter—quiet, with pruning and unanswered questions. In every season, God is not hurried. The timeline is not measured by streaks or metrics but by fruit: patience under pressure, kindness where there is no applause, faithfulness when no one is keeping score. The inner life becomes more integrated, the outer life more aligned.

Formation also reshapes our perception of the world. We start to view our redemptive work as a blessing, not just an achievement; leadership as stewardship, not control; and resources as tools for mercy. The future no longer appears as a problem to solve, but as a gift to prepare for. We begin to bring peace into rooms that lack it.

At its core, spiritual formation is God's ongoing craftsmanship—grace creating the conditions, the Spirit shaping the form, and Christ providing the pattern. We find ourselves gradually and surely becoming people who love what God loves and who move through the world with a quiet, lasting hope. We will explore in the next three chapters why our work is not worship, why we need a spiritual rhythm, and the vital role of our peers.

1

Your Work Is Not Worship

THERE WAS A SUNDAY MORNING a few years ago when Sean sat in the parking lot of his church and seriously considered quitting. That week had been brutal, and when Sunday came around, he felt like he had nothing left to give or receive. Sitting in the car, he wondered, What is the point today? Why go inside? The irony was not lost on him. There he was, a redemptive poverty worker, and he was on the verge of skipping church altogether, however, not out of rebellion or because he no longer believed. He was not feeling it.

Yet something in Sean—maybe it was muscle memory, or possibly the Spirit—nudged him forward. He walked in late, perhaps numb, but alert. A friend greeted him with a warm smile and no expectations. A child from the children's ministry tugged at his sleeve and said, "Hey, we prayed for you this week in kids' church!" The worship began, and although he could not sing a word, the voices of the congregation carried him. Someone read from Psalm 46—"God is our refuge and strength, an ever-present help in trouble"—and he felt the apathy start to break. During Communion, as he held the bread and the cup, he remembered why his faith mattered so much.

Sean left the service feeling lighter, not because his circumstances had changed, but because he was reminded of who he was, who God is, and that he was not alone. The church did not resolve all his problems then and there, but it re-centered him in grace, and the anchor held.

Sean's experience that Sunday was not uncommon but necessary. Nevertheless, more and more people in redemptive poverty work no longer feel the rhythm of the church in their lives. For Sean and many others, church had started to seem like an inefficient use of time, a luxury for those who did not understand what real suffering was. The community's pain so isolates some churches that it is hard to see their relevance at all. Some even actively avoid conversations about justice or compassion. And for those hurt by the church, the idea of returning can seem more like trauma than healing.

Good, called, and passionate people have convinced themselves that the local church is not very important. They did not leave because they loudly rejected faith. Many still claim to believe, and many continue to serve faithfully in nonprofits or ministries. However, somewhere along the way, church attendance became optional, and why? It is because the work had become worship.

A Much Larger Story

Poverty work cannot save you. You cannot outwork your soul's need for God and community. You cannot serve your way into wholeness. You cannot keep pouring out without being refilled. The primary way God designed for this to happen is through the local church. There is a subtle danger that sneaks in when you do redemptive work for too long: the temptation to make the work itself your identity, your worth, even your form of worship. You start thinking, *Why sit through a sermon when I am out here being the sermon?* You tell yourself, *I do not need a pew—I have the streets.* Furthermore, while those thoughts may sound noble, living them out is profoundly unsustainable.

Here is the truth: You are not made to give constantly without receiving. You are not God, limitless, or the Redeemer. Only Jesus is. When we root ourselves in a local church—not just the idea of church, but in a real, local community of believers—we are often reminded of this. Weekly worship recalibrates our inner compass. Communion reminds us that grace, not grit, is what sustains us. Corporate prayers remind us that we are not alone in this life. Listening to sermons reminds us that our story is part of a much larger, eternal narrative.

Your Work Depends on It

I will say this as clearly as I can: your soul cannot thrive without being part of a local church. You cannot say "I depend on God" and not be part of the very institution He established to redeem the world. The local church will do for you what podcasts, conferences, books, or social media cannot. You need a community that gathers around God—one that sings when you are silent and prays when you are numb. It is a community that holds you accountable, telling you the truth in love.

You cannot pour out endlessly without being replenished. A local church is God's primary way of providing that renewal. Do you want your work to have lasting results? Do you want to maintain your compassion and avoid becoming cynical? Do you want your work to be meaningful, not just showy? Stay connected to the church.

Now, I understand that church hurt is a real thing. Trust me, I have the scars! Some of you have been judged, dismissed, or even abused by church leaders. Some have tried to bring justice conversations into church spaces only to face blank stares or outright hostility. That is true, and it is painful. But do not confuse a toxic church with a healthy one. You might need to leave an unhealthy church, but do not give up on the idea and its importance.

Ask God to guide you to a place of healing, where people are serious about Jesus, Scripture, and justice—because such places do exist. They are not perfect, but they are present. Do not wait for the perfect church to reconnect. Flawed churches exist because flawed people do.

Seek out people who pray, love, forgive, and live life together. Yes, you may have left, but healing often begins with simply showing up again.

Faith Is the Foundation

At the start of Acts, we see a Spirit-filled community living out the gospel in real ways—sharing meals, distributing possessions, preaching boldly, and caring for the vulnerable. That is the model for the local church. It is presented as a basic redemptive institution, but sadly, we have made it much too complicated.

We forget this at times. We tend to see the local church as an institution meant mainly for critique rather than a family we choose to commit to. However, when we disconnect, we often lose the very rhythms that keep us sane and centered.

Weekly worship is not just a tradition; it is a recalibration of our lives. It reminds us of who God is and who we are. It places us in a story bigger than our latest initiative or strategy. When we lift our voices in praise, we are reminded that we are not saviors but servants. That correction alone can save us from burnout and pride.

In a world that often praises busyness, church life encourages us to slow down and take time to reflect. Reading Scripture and teaching it are wonderful, but being taught by it is even better. We should not always be serving; we need moments where we can receive. Leadership is vital, but it is equally important to be led. Humility in these moments is life-giving. Those we serve require us to be faithful and Spirit-filled, and we become that by abiding beyond our work, in worship.

If you want a clear and vivid picture of what healthy church life is, start with Acts 2:42–47 (with Acts 4:32–35 as a supporting example). It shows the church in action. They dedicate themselves to Scripture teaching, share real-life experiences, have genuine fellowship, pray, practice radical economic sharing, open their homes, and engage in community. Luke includes a line every church should aim for: “There were no needy persons among them" (Acts 4:34). That is true belonging with a solid foundation—a glimpse of heaven on earth.

Weary in Well-Doing

If the only voices in your life come from your staff, clients, or social media community, your soul will suffer. The church offers you spiritual guidance, intergenerational wisdom, and a sense of self. The work you do is demanding and can be spiritually disorienting because you are constantly giving of yourself. That is the nature of the job. Furthermore, if you are not being nourished, you will eventually run dry. The church is meant to be God's filling station. When we sing, confess, lament, and listen together, we invite God's presence to dwell in us and among us. That is not just good theology; it is good soul care.

The church reminds us that grace is not earned, that faithfulness is enough, and that the Spirit stays active even when we do not see the fruit. When we neglect being part of a church, our theology often shrinks. We might still quote Scripture in our work, but it can become just utilitarian verses used for funding proposals or staff devotionals. Without being grounded in a local church body, we may rely on our own strength and become functional humanists. However, the church pulls us back to God. It reminds us that we are not the Vine, but the branches. And disconnected branches, no matter how sincere, eventually wither.

We all need places to be human, not just the helper, the fixer, or the strong one. The church offers us that space—and not only the polished version. A good church provides room for lament, deep reflection, and wrestling with doubts. It gives us language for what our souls feel but cannot always express. If the Spirit is not intentionally shaping us in community, we will be unintentionally influenced by the chaos of our surroundings.

When we gather, we rehearse a different story. One where the last are first, where mercy wins over judgment, and where hope is not naive, but essential. We need the weekly reminder that politics does not have the final say, that oppression is not everlasting, and that Jesus rules. We also need others to walk with us, because the church is about both individual faith and communal discipleship. Others see blind spots we cannot, carry us when we stumble, and remind us that we are not alone.

Sacred and Sustaining

The church offers us rhythms of grace on a weekly, monthly, and yearly basis. These rhythms prevent us from becoming reactive, fragile, or cynical. Worship refocuses our hope. Confession of sin reminds us that we are not perfect, and that we are not supposed to be. Communion connects us to the broken body and poured-out blood of Christ—a reminder that suffering is not unfamiliar to God.

Let's approach this practically: Begin by finding a church home, not just one that meets your theological criteria, but one that nurtures your soul. Find a place where you can be known and know others—where you can both serve and rest. Make weekly worship non-negotiable, not because it is a rule, but because it is a lifeline. Read Scripture daily, not just for preparing teachings, but for nourishing your soul.

If you are more experienced, go deeper. Do not just attend—belong. Join a small group and serve in a meaningful way. Do not just read Scripture, but wrestle with it together. Let it refine your perspective, deepen your hope, and humble your leadership. When you can, bring others along and invite that coworker, neighbor, or person you have been investing in. Church is not only for us—it is for the whole world. Your presence could be the signpost someone else needs to see to transform their life.

There is something sacred about people who show up week after week. There is power in those who plant themselves in the soil of a church and let their lives serve as testimony. You may never see your name in lights, and your work might not go viral. However, over time, your commitment will speak for itself.

This is why church matters. Not because the people are perfect or because you always feel inspired, but because something happens there that does not happen anywhere else—something sacred and sustaining. It is there that God's people go to worship Him.

A Shared Spirituality

In a world divided by individualism, consumerism, and isolation, a healthy local church provides the space for sharing our spirituality. At the core of redemptive poverty work is not just a better program, strategy, or approach. It is a community shaped by a shared spirituality, anchored in Christ, grounded in the great traditions of the faith, and lived out with intentionality and integrity.

This kind of spirituality is not secondary to our mission. It is the foundation from which our work must grow. We embrace a shared spirituality not because it is easy or convenient, but because it is faithful. It is the heartbeat of God's people throughout history. Additionally, it is the only kind of life capable of bearing the weight of our calling. Let me walk you through four aspects of a shared spirituality that must ground our work. With these, we will be equipped to see lives transformed.

1. A Shared Life

Before discussing what we do, we need to consider who we are. In poverty work, it is easy to focus *only* on politics, projects, services, events, and metrics. However, we should resist that tendency. We begin with being, not doing. We start with the truth that we are not defined by what we accomplish or the circumstances we find ourselves in.

We choose to be with one another and with those we serve—not above, not apart, but as fellow travelers. Committing to church is more than just gathering. It is about anchoring our identity in a community where Christ is worshiped, Scripture shapes our lives, and we are held accountable to walk in humility and love.

We also share life with those we serve. We pursue empowerment, not control. We seek unity, not uniformity. We adopt a relational model of engagement that rejects transactional relationships and fosters mutual transformation. Poverty work cannot be outsourced, and that begins by showing up, not as heroes, but as family. Church teaches us how to do so.

2. A Shared Journey

Spiritual growth does not occur in isolation. The Christian life is not a solo journey but a shared pilgrimage. This journey is purposeful; it has a rhythm. We follow a pattern shaped by Jesus' life and the practices of the historic church—such as designated times for prayer, Communion, and observing the liturgical calendar. These are not empty rituals because, if we make space, they can serve as anchors for our souls. They draw us into the eternal story of redemption and keep us connected when the winds of chaos blow fiercely.

In a world obsessed with novelty, we choose consistency. In a culture that values spontaneity over structure, we choose rhythm. Why? Because without a shared rhythm, we risk losing connection. Without spiritual practices, our community risks becoming a mere club; our work devolves into mere activism rather than transformation, and our witness loses its power.

We are called to a deeper journey that requires us to move in step with the Spirit and in harmony with each other. Whether we pray, walk through the seasons of Advent and Lent, or take communion with reverence and joy, we see these practices not as burdens but as gifts. We walk this path together because sanctification was never meant to be a private matter.

3. A Shared Discipline

Discipline is not a popular word today. It may sound harsh and even legalistic. However, for those who yearn for transformation, it is essential. Shared discipline prevents our spirituality from becoming sentimental, reinforces our convictions, and helps us move from intention to action.

We commit to a spiritual identity built through regular, personal, and communal practices. We fast, tithe, keep the Sabbath, and go on retreat. These disciplines do not earn us favor with God; they open us to His transforming grace. They empty us so that we might be filled. They slow us so we can hear. Shared discipline also means we hold each other accountable. We do not walk this path alone. When someone stumbles, we help them up. When someone grows weary, we carry them. When someone drifts, we lovingly bring them back.

We aim for spiritual maturity, not perfection, and focus on spiritual growth that naturally improves our performance. We understand that spiritual discipline is not a private matter; it is a shared journey. It is communal, formative, and a statement that we refuse to follow the patterns of this world. In the chaos of poverty work, discipline becomes a lifeline. It grounds us when needs are overwhelming, centers us when pressures mount, and first reminds us that we are not God and second that He is faithful to sustain what He has called us to.

4. A Shared Confession

Finally, we share a common confession. In a time of spiritual doubt and theological shifts, we must anchor ourselves in something ancient, true, and dependable. We affirm our faith, passed down through generations, not just as an intellectual agreement but as a living testimony. We view documents like historic creeds not as old relics but as meaningful expressions of our shared belief in the triune God; the incarnation; the death, burial, and resurrection of Jesus Christ; and the hope of His return.

Our confession is not groundbreaking. It connects us to the rich tradition of the church and reminds us that we are not the first to walk this path. We are part of a great cloud of witnesses (Heb. 12:1). We stand on the shoulders of those who have gone before us. In our work with those experiencing poverty, we often face questions that challenge our theology: Where is God in the midst of suffering? What does justice look like? How do we speak truth without exerting domination? In these moments, we need more than slogans. We need the deep wells of Christian confession to draw from.

We do not create a new gospel. Instead, we proclaim the one we have received: Jesus Christ—crucified, risen, and reigning. This confession is not just for Sunday sermons; it is the lifeblood of our work. It reminds us why we serve, grounds our identity, fuels our hope, and keeps us focused when everything around us tends to change.

These four dimensions—shared life, shared journey, shared discipline, and shared confession—are not simply items to check off. They shape the contours of a way of life; a redemptive life rooted in the gospel and lived in community. This shared spirituality is not a side project or an internal memo; it is one of the foundations of our longevity. Without it, we risk becoming performative, burning out, fracturing, and drifting into strategies without soul.

When we live this out—when we truly share life, walk the journey, commit to discipline, and confess the historic faith—we become something beautiful. We become people marked by integrity, humility, resilience, and joy. We become people who can sustain this work over the long haul.

Reordered

Because shared spirituality reshapes our values, redirects our desires, and anchors our mission in something much more enduring than trends or tactics, it compels us to slow down, listen, repent, and cling to hope. Most importantly, it keeps us connected to God.

It is easy to overlook how radical that is in today's world. We are trained to solve, diagnose, and execute. However, having staying power in poverty work is not just about solving problems but also about sharing lives. It is not about standing above in strength but walking alongside in weakness. It is not about doing things for people experiencing poverty; it is about connecting with others in order to represent the kingdom.

Such a transformation occurs in shared spaces, where committed Christians whisper prayers and engage in honest conversations. It happens when we show up consistently for each other, even when nothing looks impressive, even when results are hard to measure. Wherever we go, we should carry a vision of people marked not just by good intentions but by a deep, shared spirituality. So, if you are lonely or longing for something more authentic, more genuine, more sacred, let this be your invitation. Do not just work for the kingdom. Live in the community of the King. The table is set. Churches are waiting. The Spirit is moving. Come, walk with us.

A few weeks ago, Sean found himself back in the same church parking lot where, years earlier, he had almost turned around and driven home. It was a gray morning, and rain tapped gently on the windshield. He had arrived early for a memorial service, as a faithful member had passed away—a quiet servant of the church who carried a rare joy. Her life had been defined by a deep commitment to the Lord and her family. He sat in the car for a few minutes, watching people arrive.

He saw the young couple she had mentored for years walking in with their kids. He saw someone he had once mentored, who had now assumed a leadership role in a small group ministry. He saw people from all walks of life coming to remember someone who was never famous but utterly faithful. As Sean sat there, he thought back to the moment when he had almost abandoned his church commitment. He reflected on just how close he had come to letting discouragement have the final word. Then, he looked out the window and saw the fruits of his decision to stay, not just in his own life but also in the lives of many others who had chosen to stay rooted.

The woman being remembered did not have a platform, but she had a pew. When the service started, the sanctuary was filled with quiet reverence. Everyone sang some of her favorite songs, which were simple, hopeful, and deeply rooted in Scripture. In the middle of the second song, something happened to Sean. He heard himself singing loudly!

He had not meant to, because he really could not carry a tune, and he did not feel particularly emotional. However, there he was, voice lifting with others, proclaiming that Christ had risen, that hope was real, and that death did not have the final say.

2

You Need a Rhythm

When you first met Pastor Martinez, he was leading a small congregation on the east side of the city. The church did not look like much from the street, just a simple brick building nestled between a boarded-up bar and a check-cashing place. The sign out front was faded, and the front steps were cracked. Still, inside, you could sense God's presence, not just during the services but in the very air. It was the kind of presence that only arises from consistent, faithful prayer.

Pastor Martinez led a church that was not trendy. There were no fancy lights, nor any social media presence. The sanctuary seated about a hundred on a good day. The sound system crackled, and the bulletins often had typos. But the Spirit was there, not because of charisma or production, but because the people—and especially their pastor—had built their lives around something deeper than relevance.

He greeted you on the morning of your first visit with a warm smile and a small leather Bible in his hand. You had learned about his community involvement because his church had become deeply woven into the life of the neighborhood. You expected to hear about programs, outreach strategies, maybe even funding models. Instead, he invited you to morning prayer.

You sat in silence for a while, then read aloud the daily lectionary reading. After another moment of stillness, he offered a short, earnest prayer, naming his church, his neighbors, and the weight they all carried without any fanfare. "People think we are holding this ministry together with good ideas," he said, "but really, it is rhythm. We keep rhythm." You did not quite get it. Rhythm?

He explained: "Years ago, I realized I could burn out trying to do everything or stay faithful to the few things that matter most. So, I began practicing a way of life that aligned with the message I preach. Daily prayer, weekly Sabbath, reading Scripture for personal growth, fasting, and practicing generosity. That rhythm became my sanity." He led you into a side room set aside for prayer and study.

It was not fancy—wooden chairs, a cross, a calendar with the church seasons scribbled on it, and a table with a notebook filled with names and places. These were things he prayed over daily. There were Scriptures taped to the wall and a worn bench he used for kneeling. "This is where I stay," he said. "Not physically, but spiritually. I come back here to stay anchored and energized."

He had been in that neighborhood for over twenty years. He baptized people, buried teenagers, counseled families, fought city hall, and hosted prayer vigils on the sidewalk. He watched church plants come and go and politicians arrive with promises and leave with excuses. Still, he was there—humble, grounded, and remarkably joyful. When asked how he managed to keep going, he shrugged. "I keep the rhythm. That is it. That is the secret."

His week followed a pattern. On Mondays, he handled administrative duties and fasted. On Tuesdays, he spent time in the neighborhood, and the knowledge gained on those days filled his prayer list. Wednesdays were for the congregation, as he mentored leaders and provided pastoral counseling. Thursdays and Fridays were dedicated to studying and sermon preparation. Saturdays, he observed a Sabbath with his family—no email, no church business, with no exceptions except for emergencies. Sundays were reserved for leading an inspiring worship service.

"It is not about being perfect," he said. "It is about being spiritually formed. I cannot serve people well if I am shaped more by stress than by Scripture." Based on that statement, you realized that, like many involved

in redemptive poverty work, you had allowed urgency to dictate your pace. Your habit of saying yes to every opportunity was not sustainable. Pastor Martinez was showing you a different model—one of lasting productivity. He had chosen a proven and reliable approach.

He taught you that spiritual disciplines are not relics of religion and reminded you how they have been used by millions of Christians throughout the centuries, serving as a model for maintaining faith. You came to realize that they remind us of who we are and whose we are, guarding us from the temptation to stretch ourselves beyond what we can handle.

He prayed because he needed to hear God's voice louder than the voices of urgency, despair, or ego. He fasted not to impress God, but to loosen his grip on comfort and stay attuned to those who go without. He read Scripture daily—not only for sermon preparation but to nourish his soul. "Before I give a word to anyone else," he said, "I need one spoken to me."

He practiced Sabbath to remind himself that he was not God, that rest was not a luxury but a commandment. A defiant declaration that neither his congregation nor his neighborhood depended on him, but on God, and that is a good thing. He gave generously because he believed in loosening the grip of scarcity on his heart. His church tithed faithfully, even when the budget was tight. "Generosity keeps us free," he said. "Stability is not built in crisis, but in rhythm." What you witnessed in Pastor Martinez was deeply redemptive. It was a life shaped by the kingdom, not by the crowd—a life where ministry flowed from spiritual formation, not frenzy.

Staying Sustainable

This work will challenge you, test your identity, push your limits, and tempt you toward control, cynicism, or pride. Without sacred rhythms, we leave our faith to chance; with them, we stay grounded and remember that we are loved before we are helpful. God's power is perfected in our surrender. For Christians, spiritual discipline is not about earning favor but about maintaining freedom.

The truth is that our sinful nature leaves us vulnerable. So, what is the antidote? How do we stay redemptive when pressure is high, needs are overwhelming, and souls are weary? The answer is not new but ancient. We practice sacred rhythms that have shaped God's people through every generation. These practices are not religious checklists but gifts. They help us keep our hearts loving, our minds renewed, and our lives aligned with the redemption we believe in. They help us resist the toxic pull of performance and pride. Let us walk through these sacred rhythms, because when practiced in the context of redemptive poverty work, they become both private devotion and public witness.

Prayer and Fasting: Breaking the Illusion of Control

Let us not just talk about dependence on God but practice it. In prayer, we remember that it is truly God who holds everything together. The most effective poverty work is faith-based and Spirit-led, not ego-driven—and it starts on our knees. Redemptive poverty work pushes the limits of our faith. The needs are profound, and the burden is real. There is no better way to maintain faith than through prayer.

Prayer is not just a formality or a spiritual checklist. It is where we stop trying to control and start trusting. Without prayer, our view of what is possible shrinks. We begin to carry burdens that God never asked us to bear. It reminds us that God is actively involved in the work. Prayer brings us back to the center, reorients our thinking, and shows us that the mission is powered not just by strategy but by the Spirit. Keep a journal or sit quietly and name what you are feeling—exhaustion, anger, loneliness, joy. Whatever is real, God can handle it. Naming these things breaks the power of isolation and welcomes God into your experience.

Fasting is closely connected to prayer, working in tandem to remind us of our dependence on God. It interrupts our habits and cravings, inviting us to remember that we live not by bread alone, but by every word that comes from the mouth of God (Matt. 4:4). It centers us as we live in a culture of excess and self-reliance.

Choosing to go without food—even for a short time—aligns our hearts with those who lack that choice. It creates space for intercession, grief, reflection, and repentance. Additionally, more than anything, it invites the Holy Spirit to meet us in our emptiness with power and presence. Fasting is not about manipulating God to get what we want. It is about making room for God, awareness, and transformation. In a world that encourages us to consume more and control everything, fasting reminds us of who sustains us and what truly matters.

Dedicate focused time daily for prayer. Even a few minutes of silence, surrender, and listening can transform your inner environment. If medically feasible, consider fasting from all food and drink for twenty-four hours every week, such as from dinner one day to dinner the next. Use the time you would typically eat to pray, reflect, and listen.

Empowering Others: Understanding Need

It is easy to fall into protecting our influence, maintaining our comfort, or pursuing outcomes that boost our image. Sometimes, without realizing it, we adopt strategies that serve our reputation more than the people we are meant to serve. However, redemptive work calls us to something better. Empowerment is not about control but about trust.

It is about recognizing the God-given dignity in those we serve and making room for their voice, leadership, and growth. It is about listening and working together, and it does not just praise good intentions—it questions, Is this genuinely helping? Empowerment is not a one-time action; it is a way of thinking, a perspective that sees others as individuals, not projects. That is where redemptive transformation begins.

Begin by intentionally creating pathways of opportunity. Empowerment means opening doors, not just offering aid. It means using your position to enable others to reach their God-given potential. Take time to assess your work through three lenses regularly:

1. *Do I understand the real needs of those I serve?*
2. *Am I collaborating with them, not just for them?*
3. *Am I holding myself accountable?*

After reflecting on those questions, do not chase a grand plan. Start with those you serve who have a visible hunger for God and with whom your influence is genuine. Quickly repent when you miss, keep a journal of what you are learning, hold on to what works, adjust what does not, and take the next faithful step.

Sanctifying Time: Healing over Hurry

In redemptive poverty work, time can feel like an unending crisis. There is always one more fire to put out, one more need to meet. We live in a constant state of urgency. However, God offers us a different way to move through time, a sacred rhythm that heals rather than rushes.

The liturgical calendar is more than tradition; it is a gift. It tells God's story through seasons—Advent, Lent, Easter, Pentecost, and others—and invites us to participate in it. It encourages us to slow down and remember that we are part of something greater than the crises we face. It grounds our current work in the eternal story of redemption.

Following the liturgical calendar can ground us. It reminds us that we are not alone, not the first, and not forgotten. We join a long line of saints who carried burdens like ours. They struggled, hoped, and persevered. Their witness gives us strength.

The beauty of the liturgical calendar is that it trains our hearts to follow Jesus by guiding us through spiritual seasons. It keeps us from living by adrenaline or circumstances and shapes us through quiet reflection instead. If you are serious about spiritual growth, reflecting on each season will develop holy reflexes over time, so that your daily thoughts become part of your daily actions.

This rhythm sanctifies time. It shifts it from something we race against into something we walk through with God. In a never-ending world, the liturgical calendar invites us to rest, reflect, and remember that redemption unfolds one faithful season at a time. Daily lectionary readings can be soul-refreshing. A simple resource I use personally is dailyLectio.net. Let the themes guide your prayers and anchor your perspective. Reflect on how each season speaks to your life and work.

Intentional Rest: Sabbath

You should not be available and accessible *all* the time. You can decline opportunities and stop checking your email after work hours. You can take a vacation and delegate tasks to others. This does not mean you are weak, but wise. Schedule times to step away from your redemptive poverty work. This is not a luxury, but something modeled for us in Genesis 2:2–3, when God rested after creating. Jesus often took time away from the crowds, the needs, and the mission. If God modeled it, we should mimic it. Make intentional space for refreshment.

God gave us the Sabbath. He commanded it. It reminds us that we are not God and that the world keeps turning even when we stop—which is a good and okay thing. When we ignore rest, we begin to live as though everything depends on us. We push harder, run on fumes, and start measuring our worth by how much we produce or how many people we help. That is not sustainable, and more importantly, it is not biblical.

Sabbath is not a break from ministry—it is ministry. It is a sacred act of resistance against the worship of work and the illusion of self-sufficiency. We are human beings, not machines. Our value comes from being beloved children of God, not from solving every crisis. Sabbath is not a luxury for when the work is done; it is a lifeline that keeps us grounded in God's grace. If we want to stay committed to this work for the long haul, we must learn to rest as if it matters—because it does.

Dedicate at least one full day each week to stepping away from work. Let it be a day of renewal and do things that bring you joy and revive you. In addition to observing the weekly Sabbath, consider taking a personal sabbatical of at least ten days each year, if possible. Step away to listen, grieve, dream, and be rejuvenated.

Generosity: Surrendering Financial Control

Money is always at the center of poverty work. We raise it, allocate it, report on it, and worry over it. If we are not careful, constant focus can subtly influence our hearts in harmful ways. We might start to think that God owes us something because of our financial sacrifices. Alternatively, we might be tempted to manipulate the stories of those we serve, shaping narratives to secure funding rather than upholding their dignity.

It is easy to let money become a measure of success or a source of silent resentment. That is why generosity and giving are so important. It is not just about funding, but also about shaping our hearts and being financially generous, which shifts our perspective. It reminds us that everything we have—resources, influence, and opportunity—is a gift. It helps us loosen our grip, surrender control, and practice trust. It keeps us grounded in gratitude, rather than entitlement and dependence.

When we activate our financial generosity, we declare that God, not money, is our provider. We reject the myth of scarcity and live from a place of radical abundance. In redemptive poverty work, generosity is not just something we offer to others; it is something we must practice ourselves. It is how we stay free from the grip of materialism.

Begin by donating 5 percent of your income to your local church and initiatives that directly help those in poverty. While not mandatory, consider practicing the tradition of tithing—giving 10 percent regularly, joyfully, and faithfully.

Years after your first visit, you found yourself back in Pastor Martinez's neighborhood. The city had changed, with new developments emerging just blocks from the old housing projects. Rents had increased, families had been displaced, and the ongoing pressures of gentrification and systemic neglect still loomed large. However, one thing had not changed: Pastor Martinez was still there.

You had not seen him in what felt like forever, so you walked into the church one weekday morning, hoping he might be there. Sure enough, you found him exactly where you expected—the third pew from the front, Bible open, head bowed. He turned and smiled when he saw you. "Still keeping rhythm?" he asked. You nodded. "Trying to!"

You sat down again in his prayer and study room, with the same wooden table and the same wall of Scriptures and prayers, although a laptop screen had replaced the paper tablet. Some requests reflected the same concerns as before, but most were new. You noticed a jar labeled "Answered" holding many slips of paper. It served as a small monument to God's movement over time. You asked how the work was progressing. He shrugged.

"Some days, it feels like the neighborhood is changing faster than the church can keep up. But I am not here to keep pace; I am here to stay faithful." That sentence carried much weight for you. In a ministry culture obsessed with impact metrics and innovation, his words sounded almost defiant. However, they were deeply rooted. He had not stopped caring about results; he had just matured in what he measured.

"I used to think I needed to be strong," he said. "Now I just want to be available enough to hear God, to love people well, and to obey." He walked you through his rhythm again, and there were slight adjustments. He now does evening prayer with a few younger pastors each week, and his fasting day is on Wednesdays instead of Mondays, but the foundation remains the same. Scripture, prayer, fasting, sabbath, empowering people, and generosity. They were still shaping him. You asked him what had changed most since you last saw him. Without hesitation, he said, "I am less reactive." That surprised you.

He continued, "The neighborhood still breaks my heart. People still disappoint me. The systems are still unjust. However, I do not crash like I used to. I do not rush to fix things I was never meant to carry. This rhythm taught me that." He leaned back and smiled. "And I do not get as tired. Not because the work got lighter, but because I stopped trying to carry it alone."

That is the power of rhythm—freedom from urgency addiction. Freedom from the myth that everything depends on us. Your visit with Pastor Martinez reminded you of something that has become increasingly evident the longer you pursue this work: the purpose of spiritual disciplines is not to make the job easier; their purpose is to strengthen us in doing the job.

They do not shield us from pain, but they keep us grounded in the One who transforms it. The truth is that this kind of work is a slow process. Sometimes, it hardly shows progress. Still, it is precisely the kind of work that shapes us into the likeness of Christ—if we allow it. And that formation does not happen by chance. It occurs intentionally and gradually. As you prepared to leave, Pastor Martinez stopped you at the door. "One last thing," he said. "The older I get, the more I believe our real impact will not be the programs we create, but the people we become."

3

You Need Peers

THEY CALLED IT THE CIRCLE, which was not very creative. They met in the church basement before the building warmed up—paper cups of coffee sending thin steam into the cold air, a plate of store-bought muffins already picked over. No one wore a name tag or had an agenda. A short prayer, a shared Scripture, and then the real work began—telling the truth about what mattered and listening closely enough to find the wisdom tucked inside.

Naomi arrived late and placed her bag on the floor as if it were heavier than it appeared. She led a neighborhood learning center that had outgrown its space and was now operating on tight margins. The night before, her board chair called with news that felt like a trumpet blast: a major foundation wanted to fund a second site, immediately, if Naomi could open by fall. It was the kind of yes leaders pray for and the kind that keeps them awake. She smiled around the table, half apology, half relief, and slid into the chair between Grace, a public-school principal, and Luis, who manages operations for a local food bank.

Mike read Matthew 25—the parable of the talents—slowly, as if the room could handle the slowness. "The master gave to each according to his ability. . . ." He closed the Bible. "Lord, help us steward what You have placed in our hands. Help us not to bury, and not to boast. Help us multiply what serves Your people." Someone whispered an amen that sounded like a sigh. Then they looked at Naomi. "It is a gift," she began, "and it scares me."

She told them about the grant: a generous, time-limited, and public one. She described the current center—beautiful, stretched thin, cobbled together with volunteer hours and miracles. "If we do not say yes, we might not see an offer like this again. If we do say yes, I do not know what might break. That is where I am. Cheerfully overwhelmed!"

Everyone remained quiet for a few seconds, long enough for the words to settle. Then the group started asking questions that shifted the conversation from speed to wisdom. Grace spoke first. "What outcome are you committed to? Not the grant. The outcome." Naomi stared at the ceiling. "Kids who can read by third grade," she said. "Families who trust this place." Luis tapped his pen. "If reading and trust are the non-negotiables, what threatens those most—space, staffing, training, or leadership attention?" Naomi thought for a moment. "Leadership attention," she said, surprising herself.

Priya, a nurse manager who thought in triage, tilted her head. "When you say, 'We are outgrowing the space,' where exactly is the choking point? Hallways? Intake? Onboarding volunteers?" Naomi laughed, a short burst. "Onboarding. We lose good people in the first month." Ben, who owns a small moving company, offered another perspective. "Marketing is easy to spend on when something hurts, but I hear you describing activation. If you doubled awareness tomorrow, would your core systems hold?" Naomi shook her head. "Not yet."

Dana, a pastor from across town, asked what she called a framing question. "What would have to be true for this decision to be easy?" Naomi blinked. "A bench of leaders I could trust," she said. The table hummed. Grace wrote her answer on a scrap of paper and slid it to Naomi: bench of leaders. She nodded, feeling recognized.

Then came the mirror. It was never harsh in the circle, but it refused to lie. "Naomi," Dana said gently, "I have watched you for a year. You are brilliant at helping others overcome their fears. When things get tense, you take on more, so others will not feel it." Heads around the table nodded, not as a verdict but as a witness. "I wonder," Dana continued, "if saying yes this fall would be you taking on more to spare everyone else again."

Naomi let out a sound that was nearly a laugh and almost a groan. "I do that," she admitted. "It feels holy until it does not."

Luis added a second mirror, kind but firm. "You do not play it safe," he said. "I do not think fear is your driver. I think being seen as faithful is. Those feel similar in the moment, but they are different. Faithfulness sometimes looks like speed; sometimes it looks like sequence." Naomi swallowed. She had come ready to defend herself against the accusation of fear. The accusation never came. Instead, the table had named something truer: a good motive that could, if untended, steer the ship into shallow water.

"Let us make it easy," Ben said, always practical. "What is each of us hearing?" Grace went first. "I hear that the mission is literacy and trust, not expansion." Priya: "I hear that activation is the bottleneck: onboarding volunteers and leaders." Luis: "I hear that attention is your scarcest resource." Dana: "And I hear a desire to be faithful, not famous." Mike smiled. "And I hear the parable. The master called the ones who multiplied 'faithful,' not 'fast.'" On the legal pad in front of Naomi, the scattered notes began to organize themselves into columns she could use.

They moved the plan forward with what the group jokingly referred to as "holy pessimism." "If this fails," Priya asked, "where does it fail first?" Naomi did not have to think. "Quality," she said. "We would hire too quickly and train too lightly. Families would feel the wobble." Luis added another diagnostic: "What will you wish you had six months after opening a second site?" Naomi answered, "Three team leads who can run without me, and an onboarding pipeline that does not depend on my calendar."

Grace shared her perspective from her experience. "First-year principals think the chaos means they are failing. It often just means the ecosystem is teaching them. However, there is a threshold—if your systems cannot carry the weight, chaos becomes damage." Everyone copied that line down. It felt like more than advice; it felt like a guardrail.

"Two more questions," Dana said. "What would stewardship look like if there were no grant on the table? And what does leadership require

of you toward the people you already serve?" The words landed with a kind of moral clarity that made the room pause. Naomi looked at the ceiling again. "If there was no grant," she said, "I would spend six months building the bench. And leadership requires me to protect the trust of the present families before I chase new ones."

Naomi pulled her notebook close and wrote her next steps in a steady hand that looked more confident than she had felt an hour earlier. "Tell the foundation: thank you. Propose a phased pilot after six months. Build leadership bench: recruit, train, delegate. Fix the onboarding pipeline. Clarify measure of quality: reading by third grade, family trust." She underlined family trust twice. She did not feel braver, exactly. She felt more authentic, as if someone had adjusted a lens she had not realized was smudged.

They prayed over her—short, specific prayers. "Lord, give Naomi wisdom for timing." "Protect the core and prepare the next." "Give her courage to say a faithful yes and a faithful not yet." When they said amen, the air felt different. Naomi tucked the scrap paper—bench of leaders—into a pocket in her purse like a promise.

The Importance of Our Peers

One of the most important ways to foster our spiritual growth is to utilize the talents and gifts God has given us effectively. In Matthew 25:14–30, Jesus shares a parable about this. In the story, the owner of a business gives different amounts of money—representing our talents and gifts—to his servants based on their ability. Their task was to increase these gifts. This demonstrates he was being fair, and the servant could not use any excuses for not trying to grow what was given to him. Making mistakes and losing money was even acceptable. The only way to fail was to do nothing, which is precisely what one servant did and was reprimanded for.

There is no excuse for avoiding what God has called us to do. He has given us our talents and giftings based on our abilities. Our time, talent, and treasure are not truly ours. This parable teaches us that our role is to manage what God has entrusted to us. God does not want us to be reckless, but He also does not want us to play it safe. Instead, He wants us to use the abilities we have been given to the best of our capacity. Peer groups are a practical way to help us do this.

No one sees the entire mountain from just one path. In our complex world, it is not a lack of information that stops most people; it is the lack of clear, trustworthy insight into what the information means and what steps to take next. The Bible calls this wisdom. For example, knowing that tomatoes are technically fruit is just information. Wisdom is knowing not to put those tomatoes in a fruit salad!

Peer groups, which are circles of people at similar levels of responsibility who meet to share ideas and insights, are among the most reliable ways to gain wisdom. They do not replace mentors, teams, or formal education. Instead, they offer a unique perspective: close enough to understand the stakes, yet far enough outside your daily routine to see what you miss. In an age where decisions are made quickly but often hindered by limited discernment, peer groups help filter out noise and clarify the signal.

This chapter is not about how to create or run a peer group. Instead, it shows how peer groups offer value—the kind that transforms a leader, stabilizes a parent, inspires an entrepreneur, deepens a pastor's impact, or helps a student see their next step clearly. Although the situations may differ, the core way insight works remains the same. Across various fields and seasons, peer groups reliably help people in at least three important ways:

They broaden and diversify perspective, revealing blind spots and reframing problems so new solutions become thinkable.

1. They deepen self-awareness through reflective mirroring, turning foggy hunches into an honest understanding of strengths, motives, and patterns.

2. They accelerate discernment and decision quality, enabling better timing, pattern recognition, and wise action amid uncertainty.

Together, these three gifts—broadened perspective, reflective mirroring, and accelerated discernment—form a flywheel. As perspective widens, people notice themselves more truthfully; as self-awareness grows, they read the landscape more accurately; as discernment improves, they return to the group with cleaner questions that yield even richer perspectives. That flywheel is the "insight engine" of a healthy peer group.

Borrowing Lenses

Insight begins with seeing more. Most of us navigate the world using a specific set of maps: the disciplines we studied, the organizations we grew up in, the mentors we admired, and the crises that shaped us. These maps are helpful, but each has gaps. In a peer group, you can borrow others' maps. When perspective widens, three things happen.

First, your assumptions are tested. You realize where you have mistaken familiarity for reliability. A leader who insists the organization has a communication problem might discover, through a peer's perspective, that the real issue is conflicting priorities disguised as miscommunication. Second, your categories become clearer. What you called a budget crisis could be more accurately described as a strategy crisis, which often requires different solutions. Third, your range of responses broadens. You shift from binary options to a broader array of potential solutions based on insights gained from peers and colleagues.

Borrowing lenses also changes how you frame your questions. Most of us approach a problem at the tactics level because tactics promise quick results. The deeper peer-group conversation often elevates the discussion to a higher level: "What is the outcome we are committed to? What constraints are real and which are inherited?

What would make this decision easier if it were true?" This shift from tactics to framing is where insight exists. When a problem is framed effectively, average options seem weaker, and strong options become surprisingly straightforward.

Borrowing lenses also embraces the tension of paradox. Complex issues seldom fit neatly into either/or categories. Peer groups help individuals move beyond false binaries to develop both/and solutions. Peers with credible yet different instincts teach each other to hold tensions instead of resolving them too soon. This fosters insight not only about what to do but also about who to be—how to lead with steadiness when the path is both contested and evolving.

Finally, perspective gains are transferable. Once you see through a peer's lens, you can apply that perspective to your daily decisions. Over time, you absorb the group's range, and your independent thinking becomes more diverse, nuanced, and resilient. That transferability is why the influence of a peer group builds up; what starts as borrowed wisdom becomes your own inherent skill.

Reflective Mirroring

If borrowing lenses helps you see the world more clearly, reflective mirroring allows you to see yourself more honestly. Work accelerates; pressures mount; subtle fears and ambitions pull from the edges; and before long, your choices are influenced by motives you have not even named. In a trusted peer circle, you hear your logic out loud, observe it in real time, and receive the gift of honest reflection. That process turns vague unease into valuable self-knowledge. Reflective mirroring provides insight in at least four ways.

First, articulation clarifies. Many people do not realize what they think until they try to express it. As you explain your situation, peers may ask you to define terms you see as obvious. Their clarifying questions bring borderline assumptions into the open. You leave with sharper language, and sharper language often reveals hidden decisions you may be struggling with.

Second, patterns are identified. Peers who have observed you for months quickly recognize your signature moves—your strengths and default behaviors. They might notice that you tend to take full responsibility for outcomes, delay difficult conversations until deadlines force them, or argue against risk while secretly craving it. When patterns are named with kindness and clarity, the act of naming itself can be freeing.

Third, motives come into focus. Few decisions are purely technical; they often carry emotional weight—a desire to be seen as competent, fears of disappointing donors, concerns about being unfair, and hopes of avoiding past wounds. Peers who care about your growth help you recognize these motives without letting them control you. The goal is not to suppress emotions, but to acknowledge and manage them effectively. Unnamed motives distort judgment; identified motives can guide judgment without taking over.

Fourth, identity becomes stable. During stressful moments, people often over-identify with a single role: the successful manager, the innovative pastor, the top student, the flawless parent. When that role is threatened, their sense of self falters, and their decisions tend to be driven by panic. Peers who value you beyond your role act as an anchor. They remind you that your worth existed before your achievements and remains after setbacks. Paradoxically, this anchoring is very practical. Leaders who do not constantly struggle for their identity in every decision are free to focus on what is best for the mission, not just what boosts their image.

Reflective mirroring often reveals that the real issue is not the surface problem. When a director believes a team member is at fault, peers gently ask, "What expectations were set?" or wonder, "What outcome are you protecting?" Over time, the director recognizes a more profound concern: a fear of conflict that disguises itself as patience.

This realization shifts how future conversations are approached and often leads to improved relationships.

Mirroring also uncovers strengths that the person has undervalued. Insight is not only about weaknesses. Many people do not realize their own excellence because they compare their normal to someone else's highlight reel. Peers might say, "You find language that lowers fear," or, "Your presence stabilizes the room," or, "You see the third option when everyone else argues about the first two." Recognizing genuine strengths leads to a better role fit, smarter delegation, and bolder but wiser risks.

Finally, reflective mirroring establishes proportion. When we are absorbed in our own story, everything feels exaggerated. A peer can help adjust issues appropriately: "This is a big decision, but it is not irreversible," or, "This matters, but it is not the main driver of your results." Proportion calms the nervous system. A calm leader thinks more clearly, listens more effectively, and acts more decisively. The insight is not just intellectual—it is embodied.

Collective Discernment

Collective discernment transforms knowledge into wiser decisions. Discernment is the skill of distinguishing what is important from what is urgent, signal from noise, and natural timing from forced timing. A peer group enhances discernment by sharing experiences, verifying assumptions, and identifying recurring patterns across various situations.

One of the most valuable forms of collective insight is vicarious learning. You do not have to make every mistake yourself to learn from it. In a peer group, you hear hard-earned stories with the underlying message intact: what people expected would happen, what actually happened, and why. Over time, these stories create a library you can turn to during decision-making moments. The goal is not to blindly follow precedent but to respect it. Historical echoes serve as a guide, not a restriction.

Discernment also improves through triangulation. Instead of relying on your single perspective as the final answer, compare it with two or three others. When independent viewpoints agree, confidence grows. When they differ, it signals where more information or patience is needed. This triangulation helps eliminate the fog of optimism and confirmation bias—the common tendency to see only what confirms our hopes.

Another form of collective discernment is timing sensitivity. Many ideas are good in the wrong season. Peers can place your decision on a timeline broader than your current urgencies. They may ask, "What has this demanded of you over the last six months?" and "What will this constrain in the six months after?" By connecting before and after, they help you see the rhythm of your commitments. The result is not only better decisions but also better sequencing: doing the right thing at a time when resources, attention, and relational capital can support it.

Peer groups also promote strategic pessimism. While optimism sparks action, pessimism helps avoid unnecessary pain. Wise groups practice gentle challenge: "What would have to be true for this to fail?" or "If this goes sideways, where will it go first?" The goal is not to scare you; it is to find weak points, and fixing them remains easy and inexpensive. When you improve a plan using these questions, you not only create a better plan but also strengthen your ability for future planning.

Another often-overlooked benefit is norm calibration. In isolation, you may normalize the abnormal or view what is ordinary as abnormal. Hearing peers describe what good looks like in their setting helps you recalibrate expectations in your own. This is especially vital during transitions—such as new roles, new cities, or new mandates—when your internal standards lag behind the new reality. Calibrated norms prevent both discouragement ("We are failing because it is harder than I thought") and drift ("We are fine because everyone is tired"). They help keep reality grounded and prevent it from being distorted by mood.

Finally, collective discernment promotes moral clarity—the courage to choose what is right even when it is costly. Conversations with peers about trade-offs, obligations, and the long-term well-being of those affected by your decisions help you clarify your values before facing pressure. When the test comes, you are not improving ethics; you are acting on convictions you have already shaped in community. That clarity is not only correct, but also effective. Leaders with predetermined guardrails spend less energy negotiating with themselves under stress. Being able to do so makes all the difference in your effectiveness.

Six months later, Naomi's palm held the warm keys. They were attached to a small ring—three silver, one brass, all labeled with strips of blue tape and block letters: OFFICE, STORAGE, LAB, EXTERIOR. She stood in the doorway of a borrowed classroom two blocks from the original center, observing the formation of the first Family Literacy Night at the pilot site.

Paper pennants hung between whiteboards. A table of library cards resembled tiny invitations. Someone had placed a bowl of clementines next to the sign-in sheet. The room smelled of pencil shavings and floor wax.

The foundation approved the phased plan, the one she had stepped out of the circle with, which she had scrawled in her notebook beside the phrase "bench of leaders." The second site would not open tonight; it would grow gradually, with two evenings a week dedicated to a reading lab for early grades, a tutoring hour for later ones, and a corner for parents to ask questions and receive answers. "Faithful, not fast," she had told the program officer on the call. "We want quality that trusts families and earns trust back." There was a pause on the line, then an exhale: "All right. Show us."

She pressed the keys into Kiana's hand. Kiana was one of the three team leaders Naomi had recruited and trained, each intentionally different: Kiana, a former teacher who could read a room with a glance; Devon, who remained quiet until it was time to insist on standards; and Mrs. Liou, who could coax volunteers into taking courage. Naomi had chosen them carefully because she wanted to give them more than just tasks to do. She aimed to give them stewardship. "These are yours tonight," Naomi said to Kiana. "You run the room. I am here if you need me, but you probably will not." Kiana laughed, nervous but bright. "We will see." She clipped the keys to her lanyard like a small ceremony.

Families streamed in: toddlers in puffy coats, older siblings trying to look unbothered, a grandmother in a floral scarf, a father balancing a baby and a backpack. Volunteers checked names, then knelt to point to letter tiles and picture books laid out in arcs. A little boy in a red hoodie traced his finger under the word "cat," then glanced up to see if anyone had noticed. Devon noticed, gave him a quiet thumbs-up and moved on. Naomi stood by the door with a stack of flyers, saying "Welcome" until the word's meaning started to settle back in.

She had not faced this alone. Since that cold morning in the church basement, the circle had been a persistent chorus. They asked the questions that turned fog into clarity. When a donor offered a larger check if she would slow the timeline, Ben texted, "Is this about impact or the photo op?" When a social post criticized the center for "going soft" because it was not opening tomorrow, Grace called: "First-year principals live in a storm of opinions. Keep your standards; keep your pace." When she felt the pull to take on every task again—"just until we launch"—Dana's gentle mirror replied: "Not fear—faithfulness. Sequence is not cowardice."

The group's cautious pessimism protected her from the blind spots of optimism. "If the pilot goes sideways, where will it go first?" Priya had asked, and Naomi answered: "Onboarding." They helped her see the bigger picture. "What will you wish you had six months after this pilot?" Luis pressed. "A way to reproduce training without me," she had said.

"Then that is the talent to multiply," he had replied, not as a suggestion but as a charge.

A small commotion drew her attention back to the room. Two volunteers had switched tables, and a line had formed at the sign-in. Naomi felt the familiar urge to grab the clipboard and take control. Instead, she stayed above the chaos. She caught Kiana's eye, nodded toward the bottleneck, and stepped aside. Kiana moved, redirected, and the line thinned.

In the corner nearest the window, a second grader read hesitantly to his grandfather, sounding out syllables as if they were stones in a river. "B-e-c-au-se," he said, eyes fixed on the page. "Because," the grandfather echoed, proud and patient. After the boy finished, he pressed a napkin into Naomi's hand with a thank-you scrawled on it.

"We almost did not come," he admitted. "I thought programs like this were for other people's families, not ours. However, Ms. Kiana called me last week and remembered my name. It felt . . . right." Naomi folded the napkin into her pocket as if it were a deed.

When the evening ended, it wrapped up like good things do—reluctantly. The kids dragged their feet; the volunteers stacked chairs. A father lingered, reading the flyer about next week's workshop on home routines. They prayed in a circle before lights out—short prayers, specific again. "Thank you for new beginnings," someone said. "Thank you for the keys," someone else added, and Kiana squeezed the ring in her hand like an amen.

STOOL LEG TWO: Engaging Stressors We Face

If you work with people experiencing poverty, you understand that the work is paradoxically both beautiful and heavy. Stress in this context is not a sign of failure; it is a natural response to a challenge. Recognizing the cost is a crucial step to serving those facing poverty effectively and sustainably.

Stress shows you care—maybe too much. The best redemptive poverty workers identify this reality and, in turn, address it. They approach stressors with a plan to manage them. They refuse to ignore or shy away from it.

Stress often manifests as secondary trauma that disrupts sleep and keeps the body in a state of high alert, as moral distress when you know what someone needs but something prevents you from helping, and as spiritual fatigue when calling masks exhaustion, leading you to carry a "savior" burden that was never yours to bear.

Unattended, these stressors accumulate. Practically, this can lead to cynicism, withdrawal, diminished empathy, and ultimately, burnout. It also raises the risk of poor decisions and unnecessary conflicts, which can harm both workers and those we aim to support.

This matters because psychologically healthy people are needed in the lives of those we serve. Your presence, curiosity, and teamwork are essential tools: stress reduces your tolerance and drains creativity. Engaging stressors and addressing them is a must. Recognizing the importance of managing stressors, those who are faithful in poverty work actively strive to maintain the right mindset, posture, and pace, as discussed in the chapters that follow.

4

Keeping the Right Mindset

YOU MET JEROME ABOUT TEN years ago, when you were still trying to understand what it meant to change the world. You were running a transitional housing program out of a converted church building on the west side of the city. It was the kind of neighborhood most people sped past—abandoned homes, underfunded schools, and corner stores with bars on the windows. But for you, it was sacred ground.

Jerome was among the first residents enrolled in the program. He did not say much initially. He nodded when spoken to and kept his head lowered. It was clear he had been through a lot and was the type of man who learned to survive by staying unseen. You offered group activities, prayer nights, and mentorship meetings, but he always kept his distance. He did not trust easily, and you understood that.

What you did not know then was that Jerome once had a close-knit family, a steady job, and a vibrant life. However, when his daughter was diagnosed with leukemia, everything fell apart. He depleted his savings, lost his job, lost his home, and ultimately lost the will to continue. His world did not collapse all at once; it disintegrated slowly and painfully, like watching paint peel in the heat. By the time he arrived at your doorstep, he was surviving, not truly living.

You started building a relationship gradually by bringing him coffee in the mornings. He never asked for it, but he always drank it. You two would sit on the steps and watch the neighborhood wake up, making small talk about the weather, sports teams, and the latest community news. He would grunt in agreement sometimes and sometimes act disinterested, but he always showed up. One morning, about six weeks in, he asked if you had kids. You told him about your family, and something softened in his eyes.

He said, "She used to love pancakes."

"Your daughter?" you asked.

He nodded.

"Pancakes on Saturdays. I would mess them up every time—too thick, burnt edges—but she would smile like it was a five-star meal."

It was small, yet significant at the same time, because it was the first time Jerome let his guard down. Over time, trust grew, not because you had answers, but because you had patience. You did not rush him or try to fix him; you simply kept showing up. That is when you started to understand that working with people experiencing poverty is about relationships, not just programs. It does not operate on schedules or grant deadlines, but on presence.

Eventually, Jerome started attending your program's small group discussions. He did not talk much at first, only listened. One night, you were discussing the parable of the Good Samaritan, and out of nowhere, he said, "You know what hurts? When people see you lying in a ditch and walk by thinking you are the problem." He added, "I am not lazy or looking for help. I get tired of people trying to fix me instead of knowing me."

After about a year, Jerome moved into permanent housing. He found a maintenance job through one of your partners. You kept in touch. He still stopped by some mornings for coffee. He started mentoring some of the younger men who came through the program. They listened to him in a way they did not listen to anyone else—not because he was polished, but because he was genuine.

Yet, the part you are most proud of is the Sunday, years after he first arrived, when Jerome came to your church. Not because anyone invited him; he just showed up. After the service, he pulled you aside. "I used to think I had to clean up before I came in here," he said, looking around the sanctuary. "But I realized this is not a place for perfect people. It is a place for people on the way." Then, he paused, looking straight at you. "You sat with me when I was in the ditch. Not to fix me, but to be with me. That is what changed me."

He was not the only one who changed. You saw how persistence in showing up until barriers fall leads to change. Jerome taught you that poverty is not about morality, failure, or personality flaws, but rather the result of compounded pain, structural injustice, and relational disconnection. You learned that the only thing strong enough to undo that kind of brokenness is a sacrificial, Christ-centered presence.

Mindsets Toward Poverty Work

As we discuss stressors, let us start with the main issue: sin. We often focus on the root causes of poverty, such as systemic injustices, and work to address them, which is important. However, as we act on these, we also need to focus on overcoming our sinful tendencies. This begins with understanding the concept of redemption. Through Christ, there is redemption from sin.

I graduated in 2021 from the Praxis Nonprofit Accelerator program, where I learned about three mindsets that shape how we serve others in the world: *exploitative, ethical,* and *redemptive.* Think of these as steps, with exploitation at the bottom and redemption at the top.

Figure 2: The Different Mindsets Toward Poverty Work

The Exploitative Step

Many of us begin, whether consciously or not, with an *exploitative mindset*. When we approach poverty this way, our work can subtly become a way to assert moral superiority. We might fall prey to the tempting illusion that we possess the answers, the power, and the resources. Furthermore, if left unchecked, this illusion can turn into a form of idolatry.

When I started my ministry in the 1990s, I met Jimmy (not his real name) and his family through a local church. He had struggled most of his adult life with substance abuse. Over time, he and his family began to find stability. Through my connections, I helped him by opening doors for Jimmy to get a job and transportation. However, one day, things took a turn for the worse.

I received a call from Jimmy's boss saying that Jimmy had been absent from work for a week. My colleague and I went to Jimmy's house to find out what was going on. We discovered that Jimmy spent the week partying. I was so angry that my colleague had to stop me from punching Jimmy—definitely not my proudest moment! Looking back, I do not blame Jimmy for my reaction because the issue was entirely mine. Jimmy was just Jimmy. The real problem was that my good intentions were centered on myself, my reputation, and feeling betrayed by him, rather than on Jimmy's redemption.

This mindset fuels a desire to control those we serve and the resources we manage. We do not need to become exploiters to fall into this trap intentionally. Due to our sinful nature, the tendency toward self-centeredness is natural—unless we deliberately resist it. This is why redemptive poverty work must begin with honest self-examination.

You might be wondering what exactly we are examining. The two main issues are control and the belief that we are superior to those we serve. We need to recognize these tendencies in ourselves first, and we must constantly weed them out because, like weeds in a garden, this mindset can easily and quickly reappear as we serve. The answer to this exploitative mindset is to replace it with an ethical one, which I will discuss in more detail shortly.

Before engaging healthily with the challenges of a neighborhood or a person in crisis, we must examine our hearts' motivations. Helping others should not be about control; it must come from a mindset that says, "I sacrifice so that others may rise." Without changing our motives, even the best programs and practices remain distorted by pride.

The Ethical Step

Moving forward requires moral growth. Hopefully, we will eventually develop an *ethical mindset* that shifts our focus from feeling superior and controlling others to challenging systems, practicing empathy, and empowering individuals. In this mindset, we recognize that both the recipient of service and the helper are equals in their humanity.

When we adopt an ethical mindset, we consider the long-term effects of our actions and ask difficult questions. We strive for fairness and oppose merely rescuing people from poverty; instead, we seek solutions that uphold their dignity. There is great beauty in this approach. It reflects the best of human conscience and the pursuit of the common good.

Many people who do not share our Christian faith live and serve with this ethical mindset, and I am grateful to God for them. They have made significant contributions to reducing suffering and promoting justice worldwide. However, as followers of Jesus, we are called to go even further. Let me emphasize that, unlike the exploitative mindset, having an ethical mindset is entirely positive. It is not a choice between being ethical *or* redemptive. Being ethical is a trait that *aligns* with being redemptive.

Think of it this way: if we see exploitative attitudes and actions, we must call them out and oppose them. However, if everyone adopted an ethical approach when serving those in poverty, whether they are Christian or non-Christian, that would be a victory. While pointing out exploitative mindsets, developing an ethical mindset is a call to action. Truly being redemptive, however, means embodying the core Christian pattern shown by Christ: creative restoration through our life and work.

The Redemptive Step

Redemption is God's costly love in action—He buys us, sets us free, and restores us to family, purpose, and a future with Him (Exod. 6:6; Mark 10:45; Eph. 1:7). Scripture states that humanity is not just misled, but enslaved to sin's power, disordered desires, shame, death, and predatory systems that profit from brokenness (John 8:34; Rom. 3:23). Advocacy alone is good, but it is nothing compared to redemption.

Being redemptive extends beyond good intentions, as having good intentions alone is insufficient in the fight against poverty. Over the years, I have seen passionate Christians attempt to make a difference, driven by a sincere desire to help, but often unaware of the deeper forces at work within themselves and the world around them. Even well-meaning efforts can cause more harm than good without a clear, Christ-centered perspective. This is because how we think about poverty shapes how we respond to it. Our mindset is the root from which our actions grow.

The Bible teaches that Christ came not only to forgive sins but also to overcome sin, death, and evil. It is God's divine act of reclaiming all that has been lost, including lives devastated by poverty. Therefore, when discussing redemptive poverty work, we are not just using religious language to describe social service. Being redemptive means connecting our work with the story in Scripture, which shows that redemption is achieved in Christ, applied by the Spirit now, and will be completed when Jesus returns. Here is what poverty work looks like from a redemptive perspective.

It is personal: forgiveness, a healed identity, and a new heart (1 Pet. 1:18–19).

- It is relational: reconciliation with God and one another; hostility dismantled (Eph. 2:14–16).
- It is both social and economic: good news to the poor, freedom for the oppressed, and repair of community life (Luke 4:18–19; Isa. 58).
- It is cosmic: creation itself will be set free from decay (Rom. 8:19–23; Rev. 21–22).

We say, "God is at work restoring the world, and I want to be a part of that." Our saying so changes everything! It humbles us. It gives us hope. Most importantly, it reminds us that we are not saviors—Jesus is. People do not need charity alone; they need someone who will come alongside them to help and, at the same time, point them to Jesus.

Our primary goal in working with people experiencing poverty is to adopt a redemptive approach, which naturally opposes exploitation and encourages ethical conduct. The redemptive mindset means our work is not about us, nor even mainly about those we serve. It is about participating in God's redemptive work in the world.

Redemptive poverty work has a vision that goes beyond merely solving problems. It aims to transform lives, neighborhoods, and systems—without compromising anyone's integrity or relationships. Redemptive poverty work connects our story with God's larger story of renewal. It understands that poverty is not just a condition to be fixed, but a brokenness to be healed, and only the power of Christ can fully restore what has been lost.

The redemptive mindset transforms our perspective, especially regarding our resources. Time, talent, and treasure are not possessions we own but responsibilities we steward. How we choose to give, serve, and what we are willing to sacrifice in the process directly reflect our spiritual condition. When faced with poverty and opportunities to serve, we receive reciprocal blessings. This framework allows the godly Christ-follower to clearly see how God has given and desires us to give in return. We are blessed to be a blessing.

One of the most important mindset shifts we can make is how we view those who live in poverty. Poverty is not an identity; rather, it is a condition that people experience. It is not who they are; it is a reality they endure. It can be easy to forget that. Scripture makes it clear that both personal and societal sin often cause poverty. Sometimes, people make choices that lead to consequences and hardship. However, just the same, people often suffer because of systems they did not create: systems rooted in greed, racism, injustice, and indifference.

As redemptive poverty workers, we do not arrive with silent judgment. We come with spoken solidarity. We recognize our own need for rescue. We, too, are in some form of poverty. There is no room for moral superiority in redemptive poverty work because we serve from a place of shared humanity. We live by the grace of God, and we extend that grace to others, which goes beyond just showing up, offering pity, and then leaving. Instead, it becomes a radical identification with those experiencing poverty. We do not look down on them; we stand by their side. Our advocacy is rooted in a sense of duty and a deep connection to their lives. We understand that their thriving is connected to our own.

This is God's story, remember? Yes, we work to change systems, challenge injustice, and build new structures, but we do so with the humility that only God can truly bring about redemption. Our role is not to control outcomes, but to remain faithful in our work. We admit when our agendas get in the way. We recognize, regret, and repent when we have contributed to the very problems we seek to fix. We listen before we lead. We need to remember that transformation is God's business—we are simply joining Him in the work.

It is not about us being heroes and saviors, but about following God in the messy, beautiful, sacred work of building God's kingdom on earth. We live in a world that is broken but not forsaken. *Poverty is a consequence of sin, and redemption is the answer.* Furthermore, if that is true, we have work to do.

Perhaps the most important aspect of a redemptive mindset is its ability to move us beyond a short-term charity outlook. While I deeply respect the role of short-term charity in helping those experiencing poverty, I aim to empower you to engage with people in poverty in a long-term way. I understand that many need their physical and emotional needs met right now. However, too often, charity for charity's sake overlooks the bigger picture. It treats symptoms without seeking a cure. When redemption comes into play, there is something far more important at stake, which is the souls of those we serve.

Short-term charity, while important, is not sufficient alone. Giving food or paying a utility bill may be necessary in the moment, but what people truly need is renewal. We should focus most of our efforts on achieving lasting restoration. This highlights the difference between transactional aid and transformational engagement.

Charity and the way of least resistance say, "I see your need and want to help you with a transaction of materialistic goods." But Jesus and the way of redemption say, "I will go beyond the transaction; I see you and want to walk with you." Neither is bad, but one is more impactful in a life-changing way. Charity is urgent but shallow, whereas redemptive poverty work is deep and lasting. Charity often begins with good intentions. Those intentions only go so far. Redemptive poverty work extends beyond our good intentions, as good intentions alone are insufficient in the fight against poverty.

Several years have passed since Jerome moved out of your transitional housing and into his own apartment across town. You have not seen him in a while, not because anything went wrong, but because, in many ways, that is the hope: that someone moves forward, finds stability, and no longer needs constant support. Still, you often wondered how he was doing. Ministry leaves you with lingering names in your prayers—faces that taught you more than you ever did them.

One day, you were invited to speak at a neighborhood leaders' luncheon hosted by a local nonprofit that you frequently partner with. The room was filled with pastors, case managers, business owners, and community members. As you walked toward the podium, you noticed a man in the back, wearing a collared shirt and appearing clean-shaven, talking to a young man. It was Jerome!

He was not just in the room, but a respected voice in it. After you spoke, Jerome approached, smiling widely and extending his hand before pulling you into a quick hug. "You clean up well," he joked. "So do you," you said with a grin. He introduced you to the young man he was mentoring—a second-chance hire from one of the reentry initiatives Jerome now helps lead. "He reminds me a lot of me," Jerome said. "But he is going to get further faster. That is the goal, right?" You nodded, holding back tears.

Later, over lunch, you both found a quiet corner, and he began to share more of his journey. He told you how the job had become a leadership opportunity and how he had started speaking at high schools, offering encouragement by sharing his story. He had recently started seminary classes part-time because, in his words, "I think God has got more for me to do." Then, without warning, he paused mid-sentence and looked you in the eye.

"You remember when I told you that charity made me feel invisible?"

"Yeah," you said softly.

"Well, now I get it. I used to think redemption meant reclaiming my life—my house, my name, my peace. But now I realize it is not just about being restored; it is about being given a new purpose."

He let that hang in the air. "That is what you always meant by redemptive, isn't it?"

You were stunned. Because, in truth, you had not always meant that.

When you started, you had good ideas that were sure to change the world, and you believed in transformation, justice, and service. However, somewhere along the way, your understanding of redemption began to expand. At first, it was about helping people survive. Then, it was about helping them thrive. But now, after years of walking alongside people like Jerome, you have come to understand that redemption is not only about making people whole so that they can walk away healed; it is also about inviting them into the redemptive mission themselves.

That day, Jerome was not just a testimony of your work—he was a partner in the effort. Moreover, that shift is everything. Because if redemption is only something we give, we miss the point. True redemption includes us all, changes us all, and calls us all to action. Jerome's story reminded you that redemption does not end with relief. It does not stop at recovery. It moves toward resurrection.

Furthermore, if you are honest, Jerome's journey reflected your own. You, too, had been on a path of redemption—not from homelessness, but from control, pride, and the false belief that people and the neighborhood would change solely because of your efforts. You had to let go of the need to be the hero. You had to unlearn the idea that good theology and good strategy were enough. You had to learn how to be present, remain flexible, and wait on God.

The more you embraced that truth, the freer you became. You no longer needed to see immediate results to believe that the Holy Spirit was moving. You no longer judged your success solely based on key performance indicators but also on how faithful you were to the task. Lunch with Jerome was more than just a reunion; it was a sacred reminder that redemption is not something we control, but a work of God.

Jerome showed you that even if someone is cast aside by society, God still sees them. And if God sees them, then you must too. That is when you started to understand what it means to be redemptive—not just ethical but surrendered. To move beyond what is good into what is godly. To do more than serve, but to join people in their story until redemption becomes possible. Jerome was a living testament.

5

Keeping the Right Posture

RICK WAS WIRY AND QUIET, with a hint of suspicion in his eyes that never fully disappeared. The first time you offered him a meal at your church, he said thanks without looking up, took the plate, and sat alone. But he kept coming back, and over time, a few words turned into small conversations. Eventually, he shared painful stories of foster homes, street corners, and prison.

There was something about Rick that stayed with you. Maybe it was the way he never asked for anything but needed everything. Or maybe it was how he never let anyone get too close yet kept showing up. Whatever it was, you decided to help him and believed you could.

And so, you went to work. You connected him to job opportunities, helped him with paperwork, assisted him in finding housing, and even vouched for him in court. You prayed with him, encouraged him, and invested your time and energy into his life. When he started writing poetry again, something he had not done in years, you celebrated like a proud parent. When he got a part-time job at a local rec center, you called it a breakthrough. You did not say it out loud, but inside, you felt that this was what ministry was meant to be.

And then, just like that, he disappeared. Calls went unanswered. He did not show up at the shelter or clock in at work. You searched for him, coming up empty for weeks. Finally, you saw him. He was sitting on a bench outside a liquor store, his hoodie up, his face gaunt, his eyes glassy. You walked over and sat beside him, unsure of what to say. He beat you to it.

"I messed up," he said. "I did not want you to see me like this." You shook your head. "Rick, I am not giving up on you. You have come too far." He did not answer immediately, just stared ahead. Then he said almost casually, "Sometimes it feels like this whole thing is more about you than it ever was about me." You sat there, stunned. It was as if someone had held up a mirror, and you were not ready to look.

You wanted to protest, explain, or defend, but did not. Something about what he said hit too close to home: he was not accusing you of not caring; he was pointing to something deeper. Over time, his transformation had become a way for you to feel like what you did mattered. You started seeing him less as a person and more as a milestone in your list of victories.

That night, when you went home, you sat in silence for a long time. It was not that you had done anything wrong, at least not in the way you usually think of it. You had done the work. However, it now seemed like you had also crossed a line without realizing it by making his healing about your own purpose. Somewhere, you started needing him to succeed more than he did, and that is never what ministry was supposed to be.

When you think of Rick now, you recall the conversation on the bench more than the poetry, the job, or any of the other victories you achieved together. You remember how his words revealed something in you that needed to be addressed. He was not ungrateful; he was just honest. Thankfully, his true words led you to realize who the real Savior is—and your way of ministering was forever changed.

Misplaced Identity

It is a quiet trap that is rarely talked about. The moment when someone's life stops being their own journey and instead becomes evidence of our own righteousness. We claim the work is about their future, but it quietly becomes about our misplaced identity. We say it is about their freedom, but it is also about our need to feel good about ourselves. The hard truth is we try to be the heroes of others' stories, forgetting that God is the true hero.

This attitude is subtle but widespread. It is not driven by malice or ego, but by a misplaced sense of identity. This be-a-hero mindset confuses the call to join God's redemptive work with the urge to own it. That is where the danger lies—not in caring too much, but in believing we are responsible for others' redemption. Others' struggles are not our scorecards. Our role is never to be the solution but to point to the One who is.

Misplaced identity does not only dwell in the people we serve; it can also reside in us as we serve. Among those we serve, stories of shame, scarcity, and survival shape how they see themselves—"I am my record, my relapse, my rent notice." However, the work can also shape us. We begin to believe we are our outcomes, our donor report, our busyness. Both are distortions. Redemptive poverty work must address identity on both sides, or we risk reproducing the harm we aim to heal.

When our sense of identity is lost, our work becomes distorted. People shaped by disappointment may distrust help, defer to authority, or accept labels that limit their autonomy and power. Practitioners guided by urgency might control processes, seek quick successes, or craft stories with impact that diminish a person's dignity. Add trauma to the mix—personal and systemic—and programs become stages where old patterns are tiredly replayed.

That is why the gospel begins with a focus on naming: God calls people "beloved," "adopted," "image-bearers," and He calls us, the practitioners and "co-laborers," not saviors. In Christ, identity is received before it is demonstrated. From that foundation, we build differently.

Savior Syndrome

A specific type of weariness sets in when you constantly try to save others. It is the kind of fatigue that not only affects your body, but also begins to wear down your spirit. At first, it feels honorable. You are showing up, working hard, and going the extra mile. However, over time, it becomes burdensome and lonely, possibly even making you feel resentful, as the results you see do not match the effort you have put in. The change you hope for has not come quickly—or at all.

Eventually, you wonder why the work you once cared deeply about now feels burdensome and empty. At the core of that fatigue often lies something more profound than overwork or stress. It is the presence of a quiet yet powerful attitude: *savior syndrome.* I have also heard it called the messiah complex.

Savior syndrome is the belief—sometimes conscious, often not—that we are personally responsible for fixing and rescuing others. It thrives in helping professions such as ministry, counseling, social services, volunteering, and missions. It often starts with genuine compassion. We notice injustice, pain, or brokenness, and something inside us says, "This is not right. I must do something."

However, that desire to serve can change over time. It shifts from focusing on our relationship with God to emphasizing our solutions, strategies, and sacrifices. We go from partnering with God in the work of redemption to believing we are the ones driving it. Without realizing it, we begin to think that change depends on our effort, wisdom, and presence. When others do not change, we often feel we have failed—or worse, that they have failed us.

Savior syndrome often appears as humility but is driven by ego. It stems from a false sense of identity, where being needed and seen as the solution gives it purpose. It lifts the helper to a hero's role—subtly disempowering the very people we seek to help.

The Weight of Redemption

The most significant danger of savior syndrome, though, is that it obscures our understanding of who the real savior is. When we adopt a savior mindset, we often think we are empowering others, but what we are really doing is making ourselves the center of their story. This can happen when someone takes control of a situation without truly listening to the other person. It can also occur when decisions are made on someone's behalf without involving them in the process. In helping this way, we see ourselves as giving endlessly without expecting anything back, and we wonder why the relationship feels one-sided and unfulfilling.

People are not projects. However, savior syndrome leads us to treat them as things to be fixed, improved, or completed. This approach takes away their dignity and the agency they need for genuine transformation. Instead of walking alongside others and supporting them, we attempt to walk for them.

Ironically, the more we try to help others, the more harm we may cause. We unintentionally foster dependency. We communicate—often without words—that people cannot rise unless *we* lift them. Moreover, we prevent them from discovering their God-given strength, resilience, and voice.

Having the correct posture changes how we serve. Instead of rushing in with answers and trying to be the hero, we adopt the posture of a learner. We start by asking questions and slowing down enough to notice what God is already doing in someone's life and how we might support that work, rather than imposing our own ideas. In redemptive work, we are not the redeemer—God is. We are not the vine but the branches. When we step into the role of savior, we take on a weight we were never meant to carry, and it is a weight that will eventually crush us.

I know from experience. I describe my ministry career as pre-burnout and post-burnout. The fuel for my burnout was the savior syndrome mindset. This does not mean our work is not important; it is! God calls us to be light in darkness, repairers of the breach, and ministers of reconciliation. However, there is a profound difference between *joining* God in redemptive work and trying to do *Godlike* work.

When we remember that God is the one who redeems, we are set free. Free from the pressure to produce results we were never meant to guarantee. Free to love people without needing to fix them. We can walk humbly, listen deeply, and trust God with outcomes we cannot control.

Empowerment over Rescue

One of the best gifts we can give others is not rescue, but empowerment. Empowerment says, "I believe in you. I see God at work in you. I trust that you are capable of growth, making informed decisions, and demonstrating leadership." Empowerment honors a person's agency. It walks alongside instead of dragging behind. It recognizes that true transformation comes mainly from within, rather than through outside intervention.

In practice, empowerment means asking more than telling. It involves including people in decisions that impact them and valuing their lived experience as much as formal expertise. It means releasing control, even when we believe we know the best course of action. Empowerment is mutual. When we stop trying to act as saviors, we open ourselves to being changed as well. We realize that we do not just bring resources, we also receive wisdom, insight, courage, and grace. We come to see that the people we are walking with are not just recipients of our help—they are image-bearers of God with something vital to teach us.

Remain Faithful

Breaking free from savior syndrome is not about stepping back from service; it is about showing up differently. It requires genuine humility, self-awareness, and honesty. It often involves doing the slow, inward work of asking: Why do I feel I must be needed? Where have I tied my identity to being the solution? How can I show up in a way that points to Jesus instead of myself?

It may also require re-evaluating our measures of success. Measuring impact by what we build, fund, or report is simple in a results-driven world. However, in the Kingdom of God, fruitfulness often shows up as faithfulness. It is like unseen seeds planted in quiet conversations, slow growth that resists quick fixes, and transformation that happens gradually through relationships based on trust and mutuality. Letting go of savior syndrome does not mean we care less. It means we trust God more, exchange control for collaboration, and re-center Christ in our theology and practice.

Savior syndrome is a trap—and a lonely one at that. However, Jesus' way offers a better path. Jesus never rushed to rescue people for His validation. He listened, asked questions, empowered, and invited people to participate in their transformation. He knew when to heal and when to let someone walk away. Ultimately, He bore the weight of redemption on the cross so we would not have to carry it ourselves.

As we engage in our sacred work, may we remember who we are and who we are not. We are not saviors. We are not the source of hope. We are simply companions on the journey, witnesses to God's power, and co-laborers in His great redemptive story. Furthermore, that is more than enough. Here is what this looks like in practice:

- *Belovedness before behavior.* We create spaces where people are valued before they are "fixed"; hospitality tables, confessional prayer with absolute assurance, and intake processes that start with assets, not deficits.

- *With, not for.* Co-design every initiative with neighbors who carry lived expertise—budget for stipends and decision-making seats. "Nothing about us without us" is a form of identity work.
- *Agency is the metric.* Shift success from service volume to voice, work, and leadership pathways—jobs with fair wages, microenterprise support, tenant associations, and youth councils. Identity grows where responsibility increases.
- *Trauma-aware rhythms.* Staff and volunteers engage in reflective supervision, set boundaries, and observe Sabbath. Neighbors receive trauma-informed care, not just referrals. Whole people, whole pace.
- *Economic repair as discipleship.* Debt relief funds, record expungement clinics, ID restoration, benefits navigation, local hiring, and ethical procurement are not extras; they are identity made visible.
- *Story stewardship.* We never trade someone's narrative for optics. Consent, dignity, and follow-up matter. Tell complete stories that include agency, not just need.

Beneath all this lies a quiet, persistent truth: Jesus has already called us by name. The cross silences condemnation. His resurrection opens a new future, and the Spirit seals our adoption. This truth applies to our neighbors and nonprofit leaders alike. From there, we move forward at a human pace, nurturing a trustworthy presence and creating structures that reveal the truth about who people truly are and our role in that story.

It had been nearly two years since that day on the bench with Rick, the day he unknowingly shared a life-changing truth with you. His words stuck with you like a pebble in your shoe—small but impossible to ignore.

They took root in your heart, transforming how you think about ministry, identity, and what it truly means to serve.

In the months that followed, Rick drifted in and out of contact. Sometimes, weeks would pass without a word. Then you would receive a late-night voicemail: a slurred but poetic stream of consciousness or a short "I am alright, Pastor. Just figuring stuff out." You did not press or chase. You let him know you were there for him. One afternoon, your phone buzzed with a text from a number you did not recognize.

"Pastor, I am going to be at the church tonight. I want to talk."—Rick

You arrived early, unsure of what to expect. The room was already half full of the usual mix—regulars from the neighborhood, a few staff members, volunteers chatting in the corners, and someone heating leftovers in the kitchen. You scanned the room, and there he was, sitting in the back. Same wiry frame, but heavier now. He looked healthier and more grounded. You walked over slowly, not wanting to crowd him. "Rick!" you exclaimed. He gently smiled.

You two sat in silence for a while, simply sharing the space. Eventually, he told you he had been in a sober house for six months and was working part-time at a local hardware store. He was writing again, mainly in his journals. No big comeback, just quiet progress. Then he said something you did not expect.

"I was wondering if you would let me pray at the end of the group tonight." You paused. "You want to lead the prayer?" He nodded. "Not preach . . . pray. For the ones like me."

There was no need for a speech. You said, "I would be honored." Later that evening, as chairs formed a loose circle and you closed the gathering, you watched Rick step forward. No notes. No trembling voice. He stood tall, took a breath, and began.

"God, we are tired out here. Not just tired from the streets but tired inside. Some of us are trying to outrun our past. Some of us fear our future. Some of us feel like we are not worth much. But You know us. You are still looking, even when we run, even when we hide, you keep showing up." He paused.

"And thank you for the people who walk with us, the ones who sit with us and see us." Another pause. He looked across the circle, eyes landing on yours because you were peeking too. "And help us not just to receive that kind of love, but to give it too. Amen." No crescendo. No applause. Just a stillness that hung in the room like sacred air.

Afterward, someone whispered to you, "Man, I needed that."

You let out a quiet breath. "Me too."

As you helped stack chairs later, you thought about the first time you met Rick—how you had tried to be his answer. And now here he was, offering something to others you could never have created: the gift of presence without pretense, a prayer born from the trenches, a testimony not of triumph but of faithfulness.

That night, as you left the church, you did not feel victorious. You felt grateful. Rick was not someone you had saved; he was someone who had taught you that helping is not about your need to be needed.

6

Keeping the Right Pace

YOU MET CARLA AT THE community center on a cold night. She was a student in the parenting life-skills class, sitting on a metal folding chair, her coat still zipped and her arms crossed like a shield. You were filling in that night because the regular leader needed to be out of town. You had no idea God was about to use her to reveal a truth you had been avoiding for years.

Near the end of the meeting, she spoke up. Her voice trembled as she said, "I am just tired of fighting for air." The room fell silent as everyone listened, and you leaned in. She continued, "It is like I have been underwater my whole life, and I thought if I could just get a little help, I could breathe again. Nevertheless, no matter what I do, I cannot seem to reach the surface." You nodded, offered a prayer, wrapped up the meeting, and drove home, but her words kept echoing inside your head.

What you did not realize at the time was that she had just voiced your soul's silent cry. You had been doing the work—leading teams, building partnerships, walking the streets, holding prayer vigils, and showing up for others as if you believed Jesus would. But somewhere in the process of pouring yourself out for the gospel's sake, you had stopped noticing how empty you had become.

Burnout does not happen all at once, and that is the tricky part. It is a gradual decline caused by many small choices—skipping rest, replying to one more email, attending another meeting, and pushing yourself past your limits day after day. To you, exhaustion signified obedience. You saw the lack of boundaries as a sign of loyalty and called self-neglect a sacrifice, convinced that Jesus would do the same.

You convinced yourself you were okay. After all, people were being helped, programs were running, and funding was coming in. However, inside, something was breaking, and you were just now beginning to hear the crack. There were signs, of course.

You had restless nights—full-blown, 3 a.m., wide-awake, cannot-shut-off-my-brain kind of insomnia. You would lie there thinking about families facing eviction, about the teenager you could not seem to reach, and about the grant proposal that was due but had not been written yet. You were way more anxious than you let on. You started snapping at your kids over small things, avoiding calls from close friends, and letting your Bible sit untouched on the nightstand. You still talked about God, but you were not really talking to Him.

Your spouse noticed it before you did and started asking if you were okay. Moreover, you brushed it off as a busy season, the weight of leadership, or just a lot going on. All of these are true, but none reveal the most profound truth. One night, you came home from a meeting that had gone late. You missed dinner again, and your youngest daughter had waited up for you with her homework, seeking help with a science project. You kissed her forehead and said you were too tired, maybe tomorrow. She gave you a sad little smile and said, "You are always tired."

Her words cut deep—not because she was wrong, but because you had become so used to being tired that you had not realized it had now become the defining feature of your life. It was not just physical exhaustion you felt; you knew you had also become spiritually dry and emotionally fragile. You were, in every way that mattered, drowning. That is why Carla's words hit you so hard.

It hit you that you were not significantly different from the people you were trying to help. You were just better at hiding it. Carla entered that room, wearing her exhaustion like a coat she did not take off. You concealed yours under layers of leadership, competence, and calling. However, still, both of you were gasping for air.

And if you are honest, part of what made you so tired was not the work itself; it was the pressure you put on yourself to constantly have the answer, to show up faithfully, and to keep it together no matter what. Somewhere along the way, you became confused about being available to others while also being responsible for them. You started carrying burdens that were not yours to carry. You forgot that Jesus was the Savior, not you.

Your slow realization sparked something as you started asking more profound questions. Not just "What needs to be done?" but "Who am I becoming in the doing?" Not only "How can I help?" but also "How can I help without losing myself?" You reached out to a mentor and admitted that you were not okay, and you began seeing a counselor. You took two weekends off in a row—a minor miracle—and allowed others to lead. You went on long walks without a plan. You reread the Psalms, not to prepare for a lesson, but to pray your way back to peace. You told God the truth and cried a lot.

What you learned: burnout does not mean weakness. It means you are human. It means you have been fighting for something important, but you forgot that the fight is not yours alone. It means you care deeply, which is good, but perhaps you have stopped taking care of yourself, which is not.

Redemptive poverty work is beautiful. It is holy ground. It is creative restoration through life sacrifice, yes—but not through life depletion. Sacrifice is sacred, but self-neglect is not. There is a difference between laying down your life and slowly bleeding out without letting anyone notice.

Sustainability is not a luxury in this work. It is a spiritual responsibility. If you want to lead well, love well, and serve well, you must live well. You need to pay attention to your soul. You must let Jesus care for you, not just work through you. The blurry line between faithfulness and burnout is not something anyone should accept as inevitable. It is something that every one of us must learn to discern.

And that discernment requires humility, community, and the courage to act.

So if you are reading this and feeling exhausted, I want you to know I see you. More importantly, God sees you. If you are showing up for others but slowly fading away in the process, if you are carrying stories that break your heart, if you are smiling on the outside but numb on the inside—there is hope.

There is a path back to rest. There is an easy yoke, a light burden. There is a God who not only calls you to work but also beckons you to abide, breathe, and belong. Let this be your permission to pause. Let this be the moment you remember: you are not alone, and you were never meant to do this alone. The work is vital, but so are you.

We rarely discuss the cost of caring. I am not referring to financial expenses or work hours, which are easily measurable. I mean the price that quietly seeps into our bones and homes—the spiritual fatigue and emotional disorientation that pervades. The feeling that no matter how much we do, it is never enough. For those of us working in the trenches of broken systems and standing shoulder to shoulder with those carrying generations of pain, this toll is real and heavy. We need a spiritually grounded, practical framework to maintain personal soul care amid our efforts. Without it, burnout is inevitable.

Hidden Burdens

One of the most challenging aspects of redemptive poverty work is that it extends beyond the task itself. It follows us into our homes and influences our thoughts, our sleep, and our relationships. It takes the form of a struggling mother or a traumatized child and whispers to us during dark hours that the world is too broken to fix and that our efforts are pointless.

There is a term for some of what we carry called *secondary trauma*. When we listen deeply to others' trauma, we do not stay unaffected. Even if the events did not happen to us directly, their effects often echo within us. We might find ourselves reliving others' pain, avoiding situations that remind us of what we have heard, or staying in a constant state of hyper-vigilance, always ready for a crisis.

Secondary trauma is different from feeling overwhelmed or overworked, but they often occur together. Overload occurs when we attempt to do too much or carry too much without sufficient rest or replenishment. Over time, it accumulates. Furthermore, if we do not take care of our souls, we can lose ourselves.

Recognizing Secondary Trauma

You might be overwhelmed or experiencing secondary trauma if any of this sounds familiar:

- You feel tired all the time, but you cannot rest.
- You often feel easily irritated, emotionally numb, or disconnected from your loved ones.
- You are not sleeping well, or you are experiencing strange, vivid dreams.
- You have begun to avoid people, including those you care about.
- You feel like you have lost your joy, laughter, and clarity.
- You resent the people you serve, questioning why you are even doing the work.
- Your faith feels uncertain, and you question God's goodness, power, or presence.
- You are beginning to believe the lies that you are not enough, you are failing, and nothing will ever change.

You may want to consider therapy, depending on how many of the above statements accurately reflect your current mindset. I want you to realize that you do not have to face this alone. Sometimes, the bravest thing we can do is admit we need a trained professional to help us untangle what is inside.

These signs are not shameful or a sign of weakness. They are messages from your soul signaling that something needs attention. Moreover, hear me clearly: caring for yourself is not selfish. It is essential. You are not just a vessel to be poured out endlessly. You are a beloved child of a God who cares about your well-being. Redemptive poverty work that is sustainable over a lifetime requires allowing ourselves to be cared for by God, others, and even ourselves.

The Sacred Invitation to Be Human

Sometimes, the exhaustion we feel is not just from the people we help but also from the pain we have never fully faced in our own lives. Our emotional wounds, unaddressed losses, unresolved trauma, and unfulfilled expectations can quietly weaken our efforts to assist others. They can distort our motivations, diminish our compassion, and keep us stuck in cycles of overwork and guilt.

We might think all we are doing is working hard for the kingdom, but beneath the surface, our hearts seek to prove our worth. We might tell ourselves we are being obedient, but inside, we are terrified of what might happen if we stop striving. We need to be brave enough to ask: Where am I serving from an unhealed place? Where does this fear drive me, instead of love calling me? God is not asking us to be heroes. He asks us to be faithful, which means knowing when to rest. Jesus Himself often withdrew to desolate places to pray, took naps amid storms, honored the Sabbath, and modeled a rhythm of rest that most of us, if we are honest, think is far too impractical to follow.

We cannot give what we do not have, offer healing when we are bleeding internally, or carry others when our souls are on the brink of collapse. This is not a rebuke but a plea. The world does not need another exhausted savior. It needs Spirit-filled servants who walk humbly and recognize their limits. So what might it look like to start over, to choose a path of healing and sustainable care? Let's remember Jesus' invitation in Matthew 11:28–30: "Come to me, all you who are weary and burdened, and I will give you rest. Take my yoke upon you and learn from me, for I am gentle and humble in heart, and you will find rest for your souls." This is not just a metaphor but a promise. Jesus does not shame us for being tired. Instead, He welcomes us. His yoke is gentle, His leadership is kind, and His rest is real.

If you are showing signs of overload or secondary trauma, it is not a sign of failure. It is a sign that you are human; maybe now is the time to let yourself be cared for, too, so you can remember who you are and whose you are. God does not want you to burn out. He wants your whole, healthy, rested self, imperfect as it is, to be anchored in Him.

Here is the invitation: start caring for your soul. You do not need to wait until you crash. Begin with a walk, a nap, a call to a friend, a whispered prayer, a pause to breathe deeply, and remember you are not alone. Let this be the moment you stop performing and start simply being. Let this be where healing begins.

It had been almost a year since the night Carla said she was tired of fighting for air. Her words cracked something open inside you, like a beam of light in a dark room. Since then, you have been on a journey of healing, learning how to breathe again, slowly and clumsily at first, like someone recovering from a long illness. You expected restoration to feel like a victory. Instead, it felt like failure. And then, one day, you looked at Carla.

She entered the room with her head held high, shoulders relaxed, and a gentle steadiness in her step. There was still weariness in her eyes, but it was no longer the kind that swallows hope. It was the kind that says, "I have been through something, and I am still here." She smiled when she saw you, as if you had been fellow travelers on the same road.

This kind of work has a high turnover rate—not just in positions but also in hearts. People leave long before they officially quit. They are still writing grants, preaching sermons, and handing out food boxes, but the light has gone out behind their eyes. You had been dangerously close to that. But somehow, God kept you tethered by grace, through good people, and through rest, which you never used to prioritize.

That night, Carla stayed after the group. You sat on the metal chairs again, but the conversation was different this time. "I used to think I would never feel pain again," she said. "Now I think it just means I am learning to carry it better." You nodded and responded, "That is truer than you know." She looked at you. "So how are you doing?" You smiled because people rarely ask you that. Or if they did, they did not want an honest answer. But Carla had earned the right.

"Better," you said. "Not perfect, not always strong. But better. I finally started paying attention to my soul. It took me a while to believe that was allowed."

"What changed?" she asked.

You thought for a moment. "Honestly? I realized I was more committed to the work than I was to the God who called me to it. I started asking: What if He cares more about me than my performance?"

She nodded.

"I used to think rest was what you did after the work was done," you said. "Now I know the rest is how I stay faithful in the work."

It felt vulnerable to admit that. For years, you had measured your worth by your output. You believed the lie that God only smiled when you were producing. But in your burnout, you met the God who sat with you in silence, who asked for nothing but your presence. And the truth is, your presence has changed. Not because you figured it all out, but because you stopped pretending you did not need help. You began to let others carry you—therapists, pastors, friends, mentors, and even co-laborers who had quietly been watching you unravel.

Carla looked at the floor, then back at you. "I almost did not make it."

"Why did you?" you inquired.

She looked around the room, then at the small stack of Bibles on the table, and finally at you. "Because in this group, I felt hope. Isn't that what most of us want?" After she left, you sat in that quiet room for a little longer. The fluorescent lights hummed. The chairs were still scattered in a circle, and you thought about how much you had changed for the better.

STOOL LEG THREE: Skill Sets We Need

If we want our calling to last, we need more than just passion. We need practiced skills that help us love people over the long term. Three stand out as essential and learnable: *emotional intelligence, community care*, and *faithful leadership*. Together, they keep us responsive, ensure that those we serve are treated with dignity, and maintain our mission's stability when pressure rises. These are not personality traits reserved for a few; they are muscles any leader or volunteer can strengthen with intention and repetition, even amid the constraints of time and resources.

Emotional intelligence begins with recognizing and naming our emotions. If we are honest, we will admit that many of our decisions are driven by emotion and justified by facts. There are steps we can take to regulate them intentionally.

Community care transforms compassion into collective action. Instead of trying to handle everything alone, create simple systems that distribute the effort, such as regular check-ins, warm handoffs, referrals, and shared goals with neighbors. Make belonging visible—learn names, celebrate small successes, and acknowledge neighborhood strengths. When harm occurs, repair quickly by listening deeply, taking responsibility, and deciding on next steps.

Faithful leadership keeps purpose at the core. It combines conviction and humility, grounded in Scripture and prayer, while staying open to feedback and collaboration. A faithful leader acknowledges reality without drama, establishes clear priorities, and focuses on what truly matters: dignity, relationships, and outcomes that neighbors helped design.

Practiced together, these skills foster a culture where people bring their whole selves, including leaders. Emotional intelligence sets the tone in the room. Community care makes sure no one bears more than they can handle. Faithful leadership guides us through ambiguity and keeps the story larger than any single program. We will cover these three skillsets over the following three chapters.

7

Community Care

THERE WAS NO INITIAL PLAN to start a community kitchen. It began with a single pot of soup. Jasmine had just moved back to the neighborhood where she grew up—a part of the city hidden away from the glossy brochures and city council tours. Her return was driven more by necessity than by vision. After a painful divorce and a job layoff that wiped out her savings, she ended up renting the upstairs unit of her aunt's house, just three blocks from where she had walked to elementary school as a girl.

It was humbling, to say the least. She had spent the last decade working for a national nonprofit headquartered downtown, developing programs that "served the under-resourced." Her days were filled with funding proposals, strategic plans, and reports that transformed stories of suffering into measurable results. But now, here she was, back in the very place she had once "served," not as a professional, but as a neighbor.

That first Sunday afternoon, as she carried her belongings up the narrow stairs to her new home, she saw Ms. Darlene sitting on the porch next door. The older woman squinted through her screen door and smiled.

"You are Jasmine's girl?" she asked.

"No, ma'am. I am Jasmine."

"Oh!" Ms. Darlene clapped her hands. "You are all grown now. Lord, have mercy. Last time I saw you, you were running around with those braids and skinned-up knees."

Jasmine laughed. "I guess I have come full circle."

Over the next few weeks, Jasmine settled in, unpacking, attending a local church, and reconnecting with the neighborhood's rhythm. However, something bothered her. Despite being close, she felt lost. The passion she once had for nonprofit work now seemed faint and tired. She had been taught to empower communities, but here, in the actual community, she felt helpless.

It was during one of those restless nights, staring at a mostly empty fridge, that she decided to make a pot of soup, not for any particular reason. She just needed to cook something that would last a few days. Then came the knock. It was Jamal, a teenager from across the street, nervously shifting from foot to foot.

"Hey, sorry to bother you. My grandma said you might have onions. She is trying to make meatloaf."

Jasmine blinked. "Yeah, I do. Want some soup too?"

His eyes lit up. "For real?"

"Yeah," she said, grabbing a bowl. "Tell her I said hi."

Jamal came back the next day with his younger cousin. Then Mr. Ray arrived, who had not had a home-cooked meal in weeks. Soon, every Thursday, Jasmine found herself making more than just soup. She would set up a folding table on the lawn, lay out a few mismatched chairs, and serve whoever showed up. The group at the table grew each week until they no longer fit on the lawn. That is when the church down the street offered its fellowship hall. They called it "Jasmine's Table." She even incorporated it as a nonprofit to accept the unexpected donations. But something still felt off.

As more volunteers arrived and more donors showed up, Jasmine started to notice something uncomfortable. They were repeating the same patterns she knew all too well. Volunteers came to feel good about themselves. They brought sandwiches and sympathy. They snapped pictures and made videos for their social media pages. They praised Jasmine for being "an angel in the community." But Jasmine was beginning to feel uneasy. She noticed how few people stayed to eat anymore.

They handed out food but did not learn anyone's name. They gave rides but never shared stories. They donated money but never asked what the neighborhood thought it needed.

One night, after the last dish had been dried and stacked, Jasmine sat with Ms. Darlene and let the silence speak.

"Something is not right," she said.

Ms. Darlene, who had been quietly sipping sweet tea, nodded slowly.

"Baby, you are doing a good thing. But sometimes a good thing can still be the wrong way."

"What do you mean?"

"You are feeding people, yes. But half of the folks who are bringing the food? They are not hungry. Not for bread, anyway. They are hungry for purpose, but they do not know it yet. And the people getting the food? They are hungry, too, but not just in the stomach. You cannot fill a soul with sandwiches."

This saddened Jasmine.

Ms. Darlene reached across the table and took her hand.

"You want to know what made Jasmine's Table special at the beginning?" Jasmine nodded.

"It was the way you listened. The way you stayed. You were not just giving people food. You were giving them you. That is what makes a difference."

That night, Jasmine prayed a different kind of prayer. She asked God to help her see clearly. To see not just needs but neighbors. Not just poverty, but people. To stop trying to save and start trying to stay.

The following weeks marked a change. She began holding community circles before meals, inviting donors, volunteers, and neighbors to talk, lead, and pray. They discussed the neighborhood's greatest needs and how to work together to improve it. They voted to create a mentoring program. Someone else offered job preparation workshops. Jasmine stepped back, allowing others to take the lead. She was no longer the face of the ministry. Instead, she was part of the body.

Jasmine's Table transformed from just a food spot into a symbol of community—where people both received and contributed. Teens painted murals, seniors led prayers, and together they cultivated a community garden. No one called it "Jasmine's" anymore. It was now known as "The Table."

Misdiagnosing Poverty

Our struggle is not due to a lack of compassion. Instead, it is because we often misunderstand what poverty truly is, which leads us to apply the wrong solutions. Although our strategies are essential and well-meaning, they tend to fall short when they are incomplete. If we are not careful, our plans will overlook the full complexity of what it means to be human, to be whole, and ultimately, to flourish. People often misdiagnose poverty when they assess from a distance, through a narrow perspective, or to save time. A better diagnosis happens when we take the time to listen, share power, and see the whole person within the entire system under the whole gospel. From that, our plans become humbler, our timelines more honest, and our neighbors' God-given dignity guides us forward.

The good news is that it is never too late. We can redefine and reimagine our response to poverty in ways that are spiritually grounded, justice-oriented, and community-driven. We can choose empowerment over dependency, systems thinking over individual solutions, sustainability over quick fixes, and participation over top-down control. Let us be the kind of people who do more than perform charity—let us pursue justice. We should see problems not just as issues but as opportunities to recognize the God-given potential in every person, because that is how the kingdom breaks in. Let me share with you five common ways of misdiagnosing poverty.

1. Neglecting the Spiritual Foundation

At our core, we are spiritual beings. No matter the economic situation, every person faces some level of poverty. This is precisely why Jesus came: to share good news with those in need and to set the captives free (Luke 4:18). He did not come to redistribute wealth or fix broken systems but to redeem us from every form of bondage.

When we neglect the spiritual aspects of poverty, we provide people with bread but not the Bread of Life. We may satisfy an immediate need but overlook the deeper wounds of someone's soul. Even more dangerously, we might act as though human flourishing can happen without God.

Jesus made a profound statement in Matthew 26:11 when He said, "The poor you will always have with you." Some see this as resignation to the permanence of poverty. However, Jesus was not being dismissive. He was reminding us that poverty is a part of the human condition in a broken world. Until He returns to make all things new, poverty will persist. That is not an excuse for inaction; it is a call for deeper engagement. It means our work must always be rooted in a spiritual foundation, recognizing the need for redemption and our hope in Christ.

If we are not careful, we might try to solve spiritual problems with material solutions. Nevertheless, true transformation does not come from what we give to people; it comes from what God does in them. That difference can change everything—from how we approach the ministry to how we design programs and measure success.

2. Fostering Dependency

We miss the target when we craft responses to poverty that create dependency. This occurs when we step in to help, but often without realizing it, all we do is take over, doing for people what they can and should do for themselves. In the name of compassion, we strip people of their dignity and self-efficacy. Our aid becomes a replacement for their own agency.

I have seen well-meaning programs distribute food, clothing, and money, sometimes for years, without asking more profound questions: What does this person have to offer? How can we include them in their recovery? What gifts are already present in this community that we are missing?

When we see individuals or communities as passive recipients instead of active contributors, we distort the Imago Dei—the image of God—within every person. We subtly but powerfully send the message: "You are broken. You have nothing. Let's fix you." However, the gospel tells a different story. It reminds us that every person, regardless of their material circumstances, has something to offer. Our role is not to rescue but to walk alongside, equip, listen, and co-labor. We must shift from relief to empowerment—from doing for to doing with—because that is where real change happens.

3. Ignoring Systemic Issues

Poverty does not occur in isolation. It results from harmful systems, unfair policies, and long-standing patterns of exclusion and inequality. However, too often, our responses focus too much on individuals. We address the symptoms instead of the root causes. We treat the injury but never deal with what is causing it.

A single mother struggling to find work often faces more than just a personal crisis. She may be facing challenges such as a lack of affordable child care, inadequate public transportation, or discriminatory hiring practices. A young man dropping out of school might not be lazy—he might be living in a community where underfunded schools and systemic bias leave him with few real options. Ignoring these realities means missing the whole picture and risking blaming the victim. We assume poor decisions are the *cause* of poverty when, in reality, poor decisions are often the *result* of poverty.

Poverty disruption requires more than charity. It calls for confronting the systems that keep people poor: educational disparities, healthcare gaps, housing inequality, and more. As followers of Christ, we are uniquely called to this work, not just as activists with an agenda. However, as ambassadors of reconciliation, repairers of the breach, and restorers of streets to dwell in (see Isa. 58:12), addressing these systems is challenging and requires time. It involves policy engagement, economic innovation, and creative redemptive efforts.

4. Prioritizing Short-Term Gains

Many traditional methods of poverty relief focus on meeting immediate needs and offering material help. We feed people now, provide shelter tonight, and give quick financial aid to those in crisis. These actions are vital—they demonstrate compassion and reflect God's heart. Yet, if we only do that, we fall short.

Relief is not the same as development. It is the start of a journey, not the end. Achieving actual poverty reduction requires a long-term perspective. It asks: What will still be standing five years from now? Will this initiative outlast the initial funding? Will this community be healthier, more self-reliant and more spiritually vibrant because of what we did?

Sustainability means we are building capacity rather than just meeting needs. It involves investing in people, training leaders, cultivating local economies, and creating systems that stay stable even after the grant ends or the donor moves on. It also requires patience. Transformation is not quick; it is rooted in and driven by steady effort. Like a tree planted by streams of water, growth takes time, but it produces fruit in its season (Ps. 1:3).

5. Overlooking Community Participation

Finally, one of our biggest mistakes is excluding people from participating in their own transformation. We design programs in conference rooms, draft solutions in board meetings, and launch initiatives without ever asking the people closest to the problem what they see. We treat poverty as an individual issue that should be solved by outside experts rather than a community issue that must be addressed from within.

This approach overlooks the power of local knowledge, shared wisdom, and collective ownership. It dismisses the gifts already present in marginalized communities. When we do not engage with the neighborhood, we miss out on vital insights and the opportunity to create lasting change. Participation is not just a tactic; it is a core value. It communicates: "You matter, your voice counts, and you are not a project but a partner in this work."

Jesus demonstrated this perfectly. He did not impose solutions from above. He walked among the people and dignified those the world had dismissed. He restored people not only through healing but through relationships. If our strategies for tackling poverty are not based on relationship and community involvement, they will never reflect the heart of Christ. Moreover, they will not be effective—not in ways that truly matter, and not in the long run.

Three years had passed since Jasmine first served soup on her lawn. Now, on a crisp Saturday morning, she sat quietly in the back pew of the old brick church where The Table now met every week. Her eyes swept a cross-section the fellowship hall, lively with laughter, conversation, and the smell of eggs, biscuits, and spiced tea. Children darted between folding chairs, and grandmothers handed out full plates. College students from across the city stood in line, shoulder to shoulder, with construction workers and day laborers. At the center of it all—a cross-section of the city breaking bread, sharing stories, and praying as if they belonged to each other.

Jasmine smiled, but it was a weary smile. The past year had been more complicated than the first two combined. Her father had died in the spring, and she stepped back from her usual role to care for her mother, who was increasingly struggling with memory loss. Others had stepped up impressively—Tyrese, now leading mentoring sessions. Ms. Jackie, once a guest at the table, now coordinates meals and volunteers. Even Jamal, the boy who first knocked on her door asking for onions, had graduated from culinary school and was helping to develop a neighborhood food co-op.

Still, Jasmine felt distant both emotionally and spiritually. In sharing leadership, she had not realized how much of her identity was tied to being the one in charge. Now, as someone playing the role, she found herself wrestling with questions she thought she had already answered, wondering if she was still needed. It felt strange not to be overextended.

A hand touched her shoulder. "Jasmine," a soft voice said, "you are back!" It was Ms. Darlene, slower in her steps but steady as ever in spirit. She slid into the pew next to Jasmine, clutching her cane in one hand and a program in the other.

"I missed you, baby," she said, eyes twinkling.

"I missed you too! It is good to be here."

Ms. Darlene looked around the room and nodded in agreement. "You see this? You planted something sacred, and now it is growing without you having to push and pull." Jasmine exhaled. "That is the hard part. I did not expect to feel . . . left out." Mrs. Darlene chuckled. "Child, you are not left out. You are just learning to let go of the superhero cape. You wore it so long, it became your skin." Jasmine looked down. "I thought I had let it go already."

"Maybe you did," Ms. Darlene said, squeezing her hand. "But sometimes we put it back on without realizing it. Especially when life gets rough, we all want to feel useful." Just then, Jackie approached with a clipboard in one hand and a wide grin on her face. "Jasmine," she beamed, "are you staying for the vision meeting after breakfast? We are planning the next season. Got some new ideas brewing."

Jasmine hesitated, and Jackie picked up on it quickly. "You do not have to lead anything, I promise. However, we would love to have your voice at the table. You have got wisdom." Jasmine nodded slowly. "I will come." Jackie winked. "Good. Oh, and make sure you try Jamal's sweet potato hash. He is showing off this morning."

After Jackie walked away, Jasmine turned back to Ms. Darlene. "You know what is wild? All the training I had, the degrees, the conferences, the frameworks—I thought that was all I needed." Ms. Darlene raised an eyebrow. "And now?" Jasmine looked out across the room again. "I think I am finally starting to believe it is not just about the strategies. There is more to it."

Keep working through the slow, messy times, when no one notices, and when you no longer feel like the expert. That was the lesson The Table had taught her. Not to save, but to stay involved. Not to deliver but to help find answers among the questions. Not to bring solutions in neat containers but to show up with an open heart and a listening ear—and let Christ do the transforming work.

The fellowship hall quieted as Tyrese stepped up for the morning reflection. He cleared his throat, smiled nervously, and then began. "I used to think I had nothing to offer," he said. "But coming here changed that. Someone—I will not say who"—he looked playfully at Jasmine—"once told me that every person has something sacred inside them. That God does not just redeem for us; He redeems through us." Murmurs of affirmation echoed through the crowd.

Tyrese continued, "The Table is not just a place where we eat. It is a space where people can be themselves. We laugh, we cry, we grow, and we serve together. No one is just a guest, and no one is just a giver. We are all something in between." Jasmine filled with joy as he spoke.

It was the very truth she had once spoken to Tyrese that now returned to her, in a complete circle, coming from his mouth. She had learned to love God's work in others, but this was something deeper. She was now learning to trust God's work, even when it was beyond her control. She sat there in awe, not because she had built something successful, but because the Spirit had created something sustainable, and she had been part of the soil.

After breakfast, Jasmine joined the planning circle. She took a seat near the back, expecting to listen. But as the team shared updates, dreams, and concerns, she found herself leaning in, asking questions, offering suggestions, and sharing laughter. It was not long before someone said, "Jasmine, would you pray for us?" She nodded, heart full, bowed her head, and said the closing prayer.

As they all rose to leave, Jasmine lingered. She watched Jackie hug a newcomer. Jamal passed out leftovers with a grin. Tyrese walked a teenager through the steps of bringing his idea to life. She no longer needed to be at the center, and she was home.

8

Emotional Intelligence

IT WAS A TUESDAY AFTERNOON in late fall, and you had just finished back-to-back meetings with community partners. Your head was buzzing with budget concerns and logistical issues related to programming. You were not exactly in the mood for deep emotional engagement. Still, that is when Manny walked into your office.

He came in like a storm wrapped in skin—fidgeting, pacing, words spilling fast. "I cannot take it anymore," he said, his voice quivering but his eyes defiant. "You said this program could help me. You said if I showed up and did the work, things would change. But I am still stuck!"

You had known Manny for about four months. He was one of those rare people with sharp intelligence that the environments around him had never been able to nurture. A skilled communicator, he could read a room better than most CEOs. Nevertheless, he carried a rage that frightened people, and rightfully so. That anger had roots deep in trauma, betrayal, and years of being passed around like a burden.

You motioned for him to sit down, but he did not. "You do not get it," he continued. "You just see another immigrant with problems. But you do not see what I am carrying."

He was right. You had not seen it yet, at least not then. You could have met with Manny to discuss policy explanations and program structures or offered a gentle redirection to the caseworker. You could have said, "I hear you," and moved on. But that day, by the grace of God, you did not look for solutions. You chose to see his humanity.

"Help me understand, Manny," you asked softly. That question made him pause, and his shoulders drooped a little. He told you about nights on the street, about sleeping with one eye open and one foot outside the blanket. He described what it was like to be twelve years old and watch his mother being beaten in front of him. He explained how every time he walked into a room, he expected to be dismissed, politicized, or even hated.

He spoke for nearly an hour, and you barely said a word. For one pure moment, you were not the program director and client. You were simply two people in the raw honesty of truth, sharing air, silence, and something sacred. What Manny did not need at that moment was a plan. He needed a witness. He needed to know that someone could hold his story without turning away from it. He needed dignity, and perhaps for the first time in a long while, he received it.

That conversation did not magically fix everything. Manny still faced a tough road, but you started to build a real relationship, not a shallow one, where you support each other not out of obligation, but because you have seen each other's pain and still choose to stay. That day became a turning point—not just for Manny, but for you.

Emotional Erosion

The real challenge in fighting poverty is not just activism. It lies in the emotional landscape of the human heart. What makes poverty so harsh is not simply the lack of money; it is also the lack of opportunities. However, the emotional damage that accompanies it—the way it whispers lies about worth, isolates individuals and families from the rest of the world, and erases the ability to believe that tomorrow might be better than today—cannot be overstated.

If we are not careful, we can unintentionally contribute to that erosion. Not because we lack compassion, but because we lack the emotional stamina to meet people where they are and stay long enough for trust to take root. I have come to believe that emotional intelligence (EQ) is not just a helpful skill for those in our line of work; it may be the most important skill—simply non-negotiable.

The Key to Sustainability

Suppose we want to walk with people through the valley of despair and help them climb toward dignity. In that case, we must become individuals who can hold emotional tension without succumbing to it. EQ is not about being soft. It is about being strong in the right ways. It is about learning how to manage our own triggers so we do not explode or withdraw when people hit a nerve. It is about knowing the difference between empathy and savior syndrome, between being present and being controlling. It is another key to sustainability.

Perhaps most importantly, it is about being able to say, "Help me understand," and truly mean it. That simple question has become a regular part of my conversations now, because I have learned that people will often only show you what they think you can handle. However, if you create genuine, emotional space, they might invite you into their deeper story.

EQ gives us the keys to that space. It helps us avoid rushing to solutions when presence is what is needed. It helps us listen without judgment, respond without reactivity, and lead without ego. The truth is that we cannot guide people to freedom if we are bound by emotional immaturity. No degree or sermon can replace the transformative power of being fully present with another human being.

I have seen it over and over—the single mom breaking down in the middle of a GED class, the teen who pretends not to care because caring has hurt him before, and the person who is afraid to trust the church again after being betrayed. Each one needed something more than service, and isn't that the true heart and mission of Jesus?

Jesus Sees Our Humanity

The Gospels are full of moments where Jesus pauses—mid-sermon, mid-journey, mid-schedule—to look someone in the eye and restore their dignity. He weeps. He listens. He blesses the overlooked. He does not just change circumstances; He changes how people see themselves.

That is the kind of work we are called to. Not just charity, but redemption. We cannot do this effectively unless we are emotionally grounded. Otherwise, we will succumb to cynicism when progress stalls. We tend to become defensive when challenged. We will start to confuse our identity with our outcomes, and we will hinder our own spiritual growth.

EQ will not fix all those issues overnight, but it will help us recognize when we are drifting off course. It will bring us back to humility, curiosity, and the kind of inner mindset that allows for growth—both in ourselves and in the people we serve. Sometimes, the most healing thing we can offer is not a solution but a safe space to feel. A place where anger can be expressed without fear, and where pain does not need to be polished, somewhere hope can take root, even if it is fragile. EQ does not make the work easier, but it makes it more human. And in a world where poverty often dehumanizes, becoming more human is one of the most radical acts we can take.

Much of what makes poverty dehumanizing is emotional: shame, isolation, chronic stress, and loss of agency. We do not want to participate in dehumanization. EQ helps us avoid that. It helps us affirm people's worth, witness their pain, and walk with them toward hope. EQ enables us to stay compassionate without collapsing, courageous without controlling, and humble without disappearing. It is not something we master once and never think about again. We grow in emotional intelligence through prayer, community, feedback, and the ongoing work of the Holy Spirit.

Key Elements of Emotional Intelligence

Mastering EQ is essential for sustainable poverty work. EQ refers to a person's ability to recognize, understand, manage, and influence their own emotions as well as those of others. The theory was developed by psychologists Peter Salovey and John D. Mayer and later popularized through several books by Daniel Goleman. It has six key elements:

1. Self-awareness—Recognizing one's emotions, triggers, and the effect of one's behavior on others.
2. Self-regulation—Managing emotions healthily, handling conflict, and avoiding impulsive reactions.
3. Motivation—Maintaining inner drive and a commitment to values, especially in adversity.
4. Empathy—Understanding and sharing the feelings of others.
5. Social skills—Building and managing healthy relationships, navigating group dynamics, and communicating effectively.
6. According to Goleman, EQ often influences success more than IQ. In redemptive poverty work, EQ is not optional; it is crucial. It is the unseen fuel that sustains our mission, maintains healthy relationships, and helps us embody Christ's redemptive character in messy, complex, and often painful situations.

Poverty Work Is Emotional Work

In redemptive poverty work, low EQ quickly causes problems. Trust diminishes. Tensions rise. Good intentions can lead to harm. Because our work is trauma related and involves power imbalances, one missed cue or poorly timed sentence can spiral—causing neighbors to withdraw, partners to cool, teams to fray, and the mission to lose momentum.

Anyone who has spent time in communities affected by poverty knows this: poverty brings grief. There is the grief of what has been lost, whether it is wealth, opportunity, or dignity. There is the grief of daily limitations, of seeing potential suppressed by systems that do not care and cycles that seem unbreakable. There is also exhaustion from trying to survive day after day.

Poverty is trauma. It leaves wounds not just in bank accounts but in bodies, minds, and spirits. For those doing redemptive work, facing such a reality means opening oneself emotionally. Without emotional intelligence, we risk becoming hardened or succumbing to the emotional burden. EQ offers us a better way. Let's examine each component more closely.

Self-Awareness: Start with the Mirror. Redemptive poverty work begins with self-examination. If we are unaware of our wounds, biases, fears, and limitations, we will inevitably project them onto others. Self-awareness involves asking tough questions: Why am I doing this work? Am I being too self-serving? What parts of my story might unconsciously influence how I see the people I serve?

People with a high EQ are not perfect, but they are honest with themselves and others. They notice when they are tired, angry, or feeling superior or helpless. This awareness is the first step to health. In redemptive poverty work, unexamined motives can lead to exploitation, even when our words sound good and our goals look noble. Knowing our emotions makes us safer, more grounded, and more trustworthy. We listen more and lecture less, creating space for others to be genuine because we are genuine too.

Self-Regulation: Peace, Not Panic. Poverty often brings chaos, with crises following one after another. People working in this area hear stories of eviction, addiction, abuse, violence, and injustice. Without emotional grounding, we tend to withdraw or react out of fear, frustration, or fatigue. Self-regulation is the ability to respond thoughtfully rather than react impulsively. It involves not taking things personally, not needing to control every outcome, and being able to de-escalate conflict rather than unintentionally fueling it.

Within a redemptive framework, self-regulation is seen as a spiritual practice. It involves choosing peace when anxiety rises, holding space for pain without rushing to fix it, and trusting God's sovereignty when everything feels out of control. When we self-regulate, we create an environment that fosters healing. Our presence becomes a source of stability.

Motivation: Driven by Purpose, Not Results. People with high EQ are motivated by purpose, not just external rewards. This is especially important in redemptive poverty work, where results are often not immediate or easy to measure. If we only focus on short-term successes or seek external praise, our efforts will not be sustainable.

Redemptive poverty work requires dedication to faithfulness even when the results of one's efforts are slow to appear. We are called to trust in people even when they disappoint us, to keep showing up when hope is hard to hold onto. This kind of motivation stems from a calling, not ego, and from obedience, not a desire for approval. When our identity is rooted in Christ and our hearts are nourished by God's love, we can do the hard work without becoming hardened or losing hope.

Empathy: Seeing People, Not Problems. Empathy might be the most visible and influential display of emotional intelligence in redemptive poverty work, and it is straightforward. Without it, we turn people into projects, make assumptions, and stop listening deeply. However, when empathy exists, people feel recognized and valued. Empathy respects the complexity of someone's story. It shifts us from judgment to compassion. It enables us to partner with people instead of patronizing them. It changes power dynamics and encourages mutual respect.

Social Skills: Building the Community We Envision. Transformation is relational. If a program is effective, it is because the people involved are making the change. People grow best in healthy, life-giving relationships. EQ helps us build that kind of relationship. It includes listening effectively, navigating conflict, collaborating across differences, and leading with humility.

Poverty work often requires coalitions among residents, funders, churches, nonprofits, and government entities. Without EQ, those coalitions can break apart under stress or ego. However, with emotional intelligence, we can communicate effectively, resolve tensions respectfully, and build trust across divides. Most importantly, we learn to center the voices of those most affected by poverty, ensuring they are not just present but empowered.

Faithful Presence

The church plays a vital role in cultivating emotionally intelligent leaders. For too long, we have focused on theological accuracy and outward behavior without addressing emotional maturity. However, spiritual maturity and EQ are deeply connected. A person who is deeply spiritual but lacks EQ can still harm.

Our churches must be places where people learn to identify their emotions, build healthy relationships, practice confession and forgiveness, and lead from a non-anxious presence. This approach is deeply biblical, and Jesus modeled it. The Psalms also express it, and Paul's letters are full of it. If we want leaders who can sustain redemption's difficult, sacred work, we must teach them how to live and lead from a place of emotional wholeness.

Redemptive poverty work demands more than skill or strategy; it requires a soul. It is not only about what we do, but also about who we are becoming. EQ is not a luxury but a lifeline. Burnout leads to superficial service. Resilience enables profound transformation. When we develop EQ, we become people who can hold pain without being consumed by it, those who can enter brokenness without themselves being broken by it. In a world marked by deep poverty, those are the kinds of leaders we need.

It takes self-awareness to recognize when you are projecting your fears or trying to control things that are not within your control. It takes self-regulation to respond to chaos with calmness and to absorb tension without exacerbating it. It takes motivation to keep moving forward when the headlines do not praise you and the results do not show your worth. It takes empathy to sit with someone in their trauma without flinching and social skills to handle messy dynamics without losing your balance. Most importantly, it takes grace for others and for yourself. Grace to believe that people can change, even when the process is painfully slow. That is the grace that will give you strength.

That is the story of EQ in our work. It is not a promise that you will never feel exhausted. It does not mean you will always get it right. However, it will help you stay. It will enable you to keep showing up when it is hard and when the progress seems invisible. It will help you stay emotionally engaged without becoming overwhelmed. Redemptive poverty work is not about perfect outcomes. It is about faithful presence, and faithful presence requires EQ.

A few years had passed since that first raw conversation with Manny. You two have shared much life since then—some good, some painful, and some that tested every ounce of patience and resolve you had. There were moments when you were unsure if he would make it.

Like the time he disappeared for three months, hiding in the shadows, and you thought he was gone for good. Or the time he lashed out at one of your team members and stormed out, shouting that nobody ever really cared about him anyway. Or the time he sat across from you, eyes hollow, voice flat, and said, "What is the point? Every time I take a step forward, life knocks me back two." Yet, there were other moments.

Moments when the fog lifted, and you glimpsed the man Manny truly was. Like when he stood proudly after finishing a construction certification course, saying he had never completed anything before in his life.

Or when he helped de-escalate a heated argument between two guys, not with bravado but with calm authority. In those moments, he showed the kind of peace earned through pain.

Or the moment he sat in a church service, clearly moved by a song about grace. Afterward, he told you, "I think I finally believe God loves me." That was the moment you realized something had shifted. Not a complete transformation, but a reorientation of the soul. Manny had begun to believe he was more than what he had survived, which is not a switch you flip but a truth you grow into.

EQ played a crucial role in making that happen, not just for Manny but for you as well. The old you might have given up on him, tried to force change faster, or taken his setbacks personally. You might have relied on control, guilt, or avoidance.

However, you have realized that redemptive poverty work is never simple but rather relational, which makes it emotional. If you wanted to walk with Manny without burning out or breaking him, you needed something profound. You had to raise your EQ. Sometimes you had to hold back your impulses and sit with his pain instead. There were moments you had to control your frustration so you would not react out of wounded pride. Other times, you had to ask God for humility.

One afternoon, long after the workday had officially ended, you found yourself walking with Manny. It had been a tough week for both of you. The air felt heavy again, just like on the day Manny walked into your office years ago. However, this time, he was the one steadying you.

"You good?" he asked.

You hesitated yet decided to make yourself vulnerable. "No. I am tired, man."

He nodded slowly. "Yeah. Me too."

You kept walking in silence for a few moments. Then he said, "But you are still here. And that matters."

9

Faithful Leadership

YOU REMEMBER THE FIRST TIME you walked into the food pantry to volunteer. The paint was peeling, and the air smelled of mildew and old fry grease. A broken vending machine blinked as if trying to stay relevant. But there was life there, with kids running through the hallways and their parents packing groceries in the back. The building was not impressive, but it felt sacred. You could tell it had weathered storms, both literal and figurative.

The people who led it? They were not the kind you would see on a stage at a leadership conference. No Instagram profiles with motivational quotes. No polished bios or brand strategies. Just faithful people doing holy work in an old, cracked building. There was one leader in particular who inspired you the most, named Joe.

Joe was a soft-spoken man with a quick wit and strong convictions. He was not the executive director, but make no mistake, he was a leader. You watched him mediate conflicts between pantry visitors, then help someone apply for housing assistance. He did not delegate compassion; he embodied it.

One afternoon, you asked him how he managed to do it all. He paused, wiped his hands on a dish towel, and said, "I do not do it all." That sentence hit you like Scripture, as he was not flashy, just faithful. And that is the kind of leadership communities need—the kind that anyone can achieve.

Flashy leadership is easy to fake. You can rent space, launch a program, and market a mission without ever stepping into the brokenness. But faithful leadership? That requires proximity. It requires time. It means showing up when no one is watching. It means learning names, attending funerals, and holding the mic only after you have held enough hands.

You once believed leadership was about charisma. Now, you realize it is about character. You once thought it was about casting vision. Now, you understand it is equally about bearing burdens. In neighborhoods plagued by poverty, leadership must take on a different form. It must be rooted in presence, shaped by the stories of the people, and attentive to real pain and promises.

You remember another time, during a freezing winter, when the boiler in the pantry broke down. With no heat and frozen pipes, most places would have closed their doors. But not Joe! He called the local church down the street, convinced a deacon to let them borrow space for a few days, and organized volunteers to drive people back and forth in their cars. That kind of leadership does not get awards, but it does earn trust. Moreover, in communities like this one, trust is a currency worth more than anything money can buy.

There was something else you noticed during that season. Joe did not just serve people; he listened to them. He once told you, "If I am not learning from the community, I am not leading it." You carry that thought with you to this day. It has turned out to be one of the most reliable lessons you have ever received.

The food pantry building was eventually renovated. However, the spirit of the place was not in the upgrades; it was in the people. It was in the leadership culture that had been nurtured over the years by people like Joe, who showed up and made small, consistent acts that built something lasting. It was the creativity that stretched $500 to meet $5,000 worth of needs. That kind of leadership does not always scale, but it does inspire transformation.

You have likely seen a similar kind of leadership elsewhere. A pastor who opens her church basement to serve hot meals after Sunday service.

A businessman who tutors after school so a struggling student can walk across the stage and graduate. A barber who uses his shop as a safe space for boys on probation. None of them call themselves leaders, yet that is what makes them powerful. Their influence is real because their investment is deep.

Leadership in these communities cannot be imported or imposed. It must be nurtured and cultivated through mutual respect, strengthened by love, and developed over time. Joe eventually retired. On his last day, the entire block hosted a cookout in his honor. There was no fanfare, just a potluck and stories. People were sad not because Joe was retiring but because a close friend was being celebrated and would be deeply missed. That is when it hit you—that faithful leadership may not bring fame, but it creates family. And in communities like these, that is what truly matters.

Rooted

The world judges leaders based on what they build; the kingdom of God judges them by what they endure. In communities facing poverty, there is much to endure. If you are not rooted in God's grace and grounded in the reality of the neighborhood, its weight will crush you. But if you are, do you have ears to hear and a heart that cares? You will discover that leadership is not just about bringing change to the community. It is about being changed by the community.

To be a redemptive presence, we must root ourselves in the community, listen deeply, and engage spiritual, physical, and relational needs holistically. We are at our best when we lead with a Bible in one hand and a broken heart for our neighborhood in the other. Leadership in these contexts cannot be distant, disembodied, or abstract.

It must be willing to repent of escapism, resist cynicism, and embrace a vision of the kingdom that touches bodies as much as it touches souls. When we lead this way, the gospel comes alive—not only in sermons but also in systems, not just in programs but in people. It becomes visible, tangible, and transformative. In doing so, it changes our communities and us.

Leadership Grows Out of Proximity

Proximity fosters compassion because you cannot lead what you do not love, and you cannot love what you do not know. Therefore, proximity means more than just physical closeness; it is relational, emotional, and spiritual. Redemptive poverty work is not just a quick outreach; it is about rooted presence. The leader who engages sincerely from the heart reminds us that God can transform even our self-interest into a redemptive calling.

Transformation is not one-sided. Yes, our neighbors benefit when we are present, but we benefit too. When we are close, we start to see the image of God in places we have never looked before. Being near helps us learn from resilience we did not realize existed. Leadership indeed matures in the tension between brokenness and beauty. Therefore, presence should serve as the foundation for our programs.

One of the most common mistakes poverty workers make is trying to "fix" the neighborhood before taking the time to feel its pulse. Presence means becoming an integral part of the place you serve. It involves getting to know the people who live there by drinking coffee on porches, hanging out at the local park, attending high school basketball games, and engaging in various other activities. Programs that grow out of presence are always better than those imposed from a distance. They are more responsive, more sustainable, and more empowering. People want neighbors and friends more than they want saviors.

When we lead as rooted leaders, we become inspiring because our organizations reflect our leadership. If leaders are unreachable, the organization tends to become isolated and stagnant. However, when leaders participate in community cleanups, public forums, and family cookouts, the neighborhood takes notice. They realize that being part of the organization is not just about staying behind the scenes but about demonstrating their faith openly.

A rooted leader fosters bravery within the organization. People will start to believe they belong, that they matter, and that they can act as agents of change in their communities. This shift—from spectators to stakeholders—is one of the most powerful things a leader can nurture.

Leadership Reflects the Kingdom of God

The kingdom must be shown, not just announced. We have too many leaders and organizations trying to sell a gospel they have not experienced. The kingdom of God is not just a brand to promote, but an actual reality. That is what Jesus meant when He said the kingdom is like yeast worked through dough (Luke 13:20–21). It is slow and subtle, but it changes everything. We need to resist the urge to worship at the altar of visibility and instead seek credibility by remaining quietly faithful.

Whether it is a tutoring program that considers kids as learners or a recovery group that revitalizes those battling addiction, kingdom leadership reveals itself in visible ways. We share the gospel with our words, yes—but we also show it through the meals we provide, the injustices we fight against, and the hope we carry.

The gospel is holistic because the spiritual and material are not enemies; they are dance partners in God's mission. Holistic leadership does not mean watering down the gospel; it means expanding the understanding of what salvation includes. Jesus healed the sick and forgave sin in the same breath. He multiplied loaves and exposed corrupt power structures. Our gospel must be as complete as our Christ. In our settings, this holistic vision means challenging injustice, not replacing the gospel, but because of it.

Christians are a prophetic presence. We must carry a prophetic voice in both the public square and the pulpit. That does not mean being political in a partisan sense. It means having the courage to speak God's truth into the brokenness of society. The prophet does not just say, "That is wrong." Instead, they say, "This is what the kingdom looks like."

Prophetic leadership fosters alternative economies of grace. It embraces the undocumented. It openly recognizes racism. It supports local businesses. It treats people with dignity and helps them realize their worth. When we lead in this way, we will not only build organizations but also ignite movements.

The kingdom confronts and comforts. Communities facing poverty carry the weight of generational trauma, systemic inequality, and daily struggles for survival. Kingdom leaders must know how to both challenge injustice and comfort those who are suffering. That is what Jesus did—He overturned tables in the temple and gently fed the hungry. He called out the Pharisees and restored dignity to those society had cast aside.

For us, this involves learning to read both the Bible and the block. It means showing up in times of crisis and celebration. It includes calling out injustice—not just with words but also by advocating for policies that dismantle those realities. It also involves cultivating an organizational culture where people feel seen and safe, making our organizations a refuge.

Kingdom vision helps shape our priorities. We all face resource limitations, such as financial constraints and staff shortages. However, if we have a kingdom vision, we know we have the resources to make a difference. The goal is not to be the most polished organization, but a faithful one. It also clarifies decision-making.

Start by asking: Does this program reflect Jesus' heart for people experiencing poverty? Does this budget line empower our neighbors or entertain our donors? Does our communication reflect and address what our people are living through? Organizations that reflect the kingdom care about numbers, yes, but they are more concerned about the impact they have on communities and the people in them.

Leadership Comes from the Inside Out

Repentance is the starting point. We are not immune to the temptations of platform, performance, and prestige. Redemptive poverty work can sometimes feel like a grind, and the temptation to disengage or act out of ego is very real. That is why repentance is not a one-time act—it is a rhythm. Redemptive leaders continually ask, "Lord, search me." They return to the feet of Jesus, not to perform, but to be purified.

Repentance influences how we discuss poverty. With a repentant heart, we can stop blaming the community for its issues and begin to examine how our fears or comforts may have led to inaction. We move from criticism to confession, and by doing so, earn moral authority not from our perfection but from our honesty.

Leadership is built from the crucible of community. Redemptive poverty work is not glamorous; it is shaped in the grit of life. It happens when your daily plans get interrupted by an emergency call, when someone you discipled falls back into addiction, or when you baptize someone in the morning and mourn a homicide in the evening.

This is where genuine leaders are shaped—not in conference rooms but within the community, not on social media but through hospital visits. Our work pushes us beyond our limits and encourages us to rely on God. While this work will reveal your idols, it will also strengthen your relationship with the Holy Spirit.

I want to remind you that our private lives support our public work. We face spiritual warfare in unseen yet deeply felt ways. The violence in your neighborhood, the ancestral wounds within your community, and the loneliness in your own heart—all of these build up. That is why internal spiritual growth is not optional; it is your lifeline. The work will drain you, but the Spirit will sustain you as long as you make space for it. I have seen too many good leaders burn out because they give everything to others and nothing to their souls.

Do not confuse burnout with sacrifice. Jesus laid His life down—He did not burn it out. There is a difference; learn this lesson before it is too late.

Accountability keeps us grounded. One of the hidden dangers in our work is the risk of isolation. When you are doing something that feels pioneering or sacrificial, it is easy to start thinking that no one understands you, which is a dangerous mindset. We all need peers who can ask tough questions and speak the truth with kindness.

You need someone who can tell you when you are veering off course. Someone who cares more about your soul than your success. In our work, this becomes even more important because the margin for error is often slim. You cannot afford to lead without a community that supports you and keeps you accountable.

This can involve finding a network of supportive people, exercising regularly, joining a healthy church, or meeting monthly with a spiritual director. Do whatever is necessary to take care of yourself because your internal life will always influence your external leadership.

Leadership grows through authenticity. You do not have to be impressive; just genuine. People can tell a fake from miles away, especially in the communities we serve. They have been through too much to be fooled by surface-level polish. They want leaders who bleed, love deeply, and tell the truth even when it costs them.

Authentic leadership grows because it allows others to be their true selves. It fosters a culture where vulnerability is a sign of strength and healing can happen. When we lead from our scars rather than our résumés, people will be attracted to redemption.

Some days, it feels like you are planting a garden in concrete. If you are a pastor, you will preach your heart out and wonder if the Word made any impact. If you lead a nonprofit, you will plan programs that only a few attend. If you are a volunteer, you will invest in people who seem to disappear overnight. We all pray over budgets that do not add up and buildings that keep falling apart. Nevertheless, we are still expected to smile, to lead, to shepherd. But keep going!

Let Us Not Grow Weary in Well-Doing

Even when you are tired, what you are doing remains sacred. The seeds you plant in difficult soil may take time to grow, but they are not planted in vain. God notices them. They are the kind of seeds heaven cherishes—seeds of faithfulness, presence, and sacrificial love. They are watered by your tears and nourished by your obedience, and eventually, they will produce a harvest that is both wide and deep.

Yes, there will be days when you wonder if it is worth it. You will grieve and lament. You will sit with people in their darkest moments and still be expected to carry light. You will confront systems that seem immovable. You will disciple folks who may disappear or disappoint. And then, you will do it all over again, sometimes from a place of weariness so deep it borders on despair.

But even then—especially then—your faithfulness matters. Every meal you serve, every kid you affirm, every prayer you whisper while walking down the block—God sees it! He honors it. His Spirit moves through it. You are not wasting your efforts. You are partnering with the God who raises the dead and brings beauty from ashes.

And when your strength diminishes, remember: you are not the savior. That burden is too heavy for your shoulders to bear. It was never meant for you. Our communities belong to God. He was working before you arrived, and He will still be working long after you are gone. He loves your community more than you ever could. You are not the Messiah, but you are His messenger. So take a deep breath, release the burden, and keep moving forward.

Know that you are not alone. You are part of a faithful remnant of redemptive poverty workers who embody the gospel one block at a time. You belong to a long line of saints who refuse to abandon the neighborhood, who trade applause for proximity, and who believe that broken places are still holy ground.

Together, we are creating something beautiful. It might not make headlines or win awards, but it will endure because it is built on the cornerstone of Christ. So keep showing up. Keep loving deeply. Keep planting, even in concrete, because resurrection does not only happen in empty tombs. It happens in communities like the one you are called to. Moreover, you, my friend, are part of the redemption.

A few years after Joe retired, you received a call from the young leader who had taken his place, Juanita. As a long-time former volunteer, she was encouraged to reach out to you. She had interned at the pantry during college and eventually came back to serve full-time. She had the same kind of fire that reminded you of when you volunteered there—ambitious, idealistic, eager to make a difference. She told you she still hears stories about Joe, but it frustrates her because she feels she could never be the kind of leader he was.

You met her at a corner cafe just a block from the pantry. It is ironic because that cafe used to be a boarded-up building. Now, it has refurbished wood tables, exposed brick, and overpriced coffee. Gentrification had crept in like a fog—quiet but unmistakable. Juanita walked in wearing a hoodie with the pantry's logo, and you could tell by the bags under her eyes that the work had started to weigh on her. She sat down, barely touched her drink, and exhaled as if she had been running on a treadmill.

"I am doing everything I know to do," she said. "The food pantry's expanded; we are even running job readiness workshops now. However, I feel like I am losing touch with the community. People still smile when they see me, but it is as if the connection is no longer there. Not like it was when Joe was there." You listened intently, as you are now a wise veteran.

Then you asked her, "When is the last time you sat on someone's porch to talk? No agenda and no program to pitch. Just presence?" She blinked as if she were trying to remember. She replied, "Honestly? I do not know. I have been so caught up in keeping things running that I have not had the margin."

That is when you shared a lesson Joe once taught you. "Programs do not make a presence. Presence makes programs. You cannot schedule your way into people's hearts. You have to be with them." She nodded slowly as you poured into her everything Joe had poured into you.

You talked for over an hour. You shared the insights gained from on-the-job experience and reminded her that the most important thing she could offer was not her efficiency, but her faithfulness.

"People trusted Joe," you told her, "because he did not lead from above them. He led among them and knew their stories. He remembered birthdays and prayed with mothers in hospital waiting rooms. He did not just build a pantry—he built a space to belong." "I want that," she said. "But I am scared I am not enough." And you told her the truth: "You are not."

She looked at you, startled, until you added, "You are not supposed to be. That is not a failure. That is your freedom. You are not the savior; you are the seed planter. That is what faithful leaders do. We sow, we water, and we trust God with the growth." She smiled, the kind of smile that holds both surrender and strength.

Juanita symbolizes a new wave of leaders stepping into old roles, facing fresh challenges, as they enter neighborhoods transformed by factors like gentrification. They inherit institutions with shaky budgets and even shakier trust. They also feel the pressure to prove they belong while wondering if they will survive the journey.

But you saw something in Juanita that day—a spark of resolve, a willingness to slow down, to dig in, and to lead not from her accomplishments but from her character. And that is what gives you hope—not just for her, but for every leader showing up in tough places with trembling hands and sincere hearts.

A few months later, you attended the food pantry's Thanksgiving celebration meal. It had always been Joe's favorite event. You remember how he used to fuss about the bouncy house being lopsided or the turkey being too dry. Still, it was never about perfection. It was about people feeling safe, seen, and at home.

When you walked onto the lot, you noticed a few changes. There was new signage, an improved sound system, and even a pop-up booth promoting local entrepreneurs. However, what moved you most was not any of that—it was Juanita, standing near the entrance, holding a cup of hot cider, listening attentively to a mother share her son's recent struggle with depression. She was not rushing to finish her tasks or checking her phone. She was truly present.

Conclusion

You have completed the entire journey of this book—discovering the hidden stressors that drain the soul, the skills that turn care into action, and the spiritual practices that keep us rooted in Christ. Redemptive poverty work is not just a single method or program; it is a perspective, a way of being, and a way of building—so that people made in God's image can flourish both physically and spiritually. This way, those who serve do not lose themselves while loving their neighbors.

If you remember only one thing, remember this: people, not programs, are God's chosen vessels for redemption. You are one of those people, not because you can carry everything, but because you are called. The people you serve are not problems to be solved; they are partners to be honored. Your limits are not obstacles to avoid; instead, they are opportunities for growth and development. Your work is not the point; Jesus is. However, in His hands, your work becomes bread for the hungry, a door for the excluded, a bridge over old wounds, even a song children dance to because their parents have found peace.

So go as a hopeful realist! Go in peace. Go as a neighbor among neighbors. Go as a steward of power. Go as a person who rests. Go with:

The spiritual growth that protects your heart from idolizing the work you do.

- The rhythm that energizes your soul.
- The peers who turn knowledge into wisdom.
- The mindset that combines truth with hope.

- The posture that respects dignity before finding solutions.
- The pace that keeps you human.
- The skills that turn compassion into action.

Take courage! Keep your stool strong. May the Spirit make you wise, the Son make you brave, and the Father keep you compassionate. May your "yes" be an echo of His, your "no" a guardrail of self-care, and your ordinary days the place where miracles grow.

APPENDIX: A Brief Theological Reflection

Whatever situation we choose to engage in, the first step should always be to find out what the Bible says about it. When it comes to those in poverty, this step is often overlooked for some reason. This should not be the case. The Bible offers significant guidance on how to treat those in poverty. I will briefly discuss Old Testament principles of empowerment and then highlight two key aspects of Jesus' teachings: He favored the poor and warned against the love of riches.

Empowerment

Empowering someone means offering opportunities to help improve their situation. In the Old Testament, we see that:

Extraordinary attention was to be given toward making sure justice was found for those who were poor (Exod. 23:6; Amos 5:12; Ps. 10:2, 9).

- At all times, some fruit and vegetables were to be left in the fields for the poor to gather (Lev. 19:9–10).
- No interest was to be charged on loans to those in poverty (Exod. 22:25).
- Every three years a tithe was to be made to orphans and widows (Deut. 14:28–29).

- Every seven years farm fields were to rest and not be used for profit but rather for those less fortunate to gather what grew naturally for themselves (Exod. 23:10–11; Lev. 25:3–6).
- Slaves were to be freed after six years of service (Exod. 21:2).
- Every fiftieth year (Year of Jubilee) lands were to revert to their original owners (Lev. 25:8–17).

Jesus Favored the Poor

We see Christ's special concern for the poor in His earthly ministry. During His time on earth, Jesus carried out His ministry as a humble, ordinary person. Biblical historians tell us that His hometown of Nazareth was not viewed favorably. His birth in a stable reflected the poverty of His circumstances. Jesus entered and lived in the world in the humblest, most ordinary way imaginable.

As we anticipate Christ's second coming, we must remember His commands to stay prepared for His return and to serve the poor as He did. Eventually, we will need to stand before our Lord and demonstrate how we treated the poor during our lives (see Matt. 25:31–46). We must provide evidence of our efforts to create opportunities for those living in poverty.

In Matthew 25:35–36, Jesus equates caring for those who are hungry, thirsty, strangers, naked, sick, or in prison with caring for Him. If we accept His words, this offers a powerful lesson. If you are not dedicating parts of your life, mission, and resources to help those in poverty, begin doing so right away. This is not about earning salvation but about living in response to the grace Christ has shown us.

Jesus Warned Against Riches

Our spiritual state and how we view money are connected, so our resource-related decisions matter a lot. During Christ's time on earth, a common false belief was that being wealthy guaranteed salvation. Jesus strongly taught against this idea (Matt. 19:23–30).

According to Matthew 6:24, money is the main thing we need to guard against turning into an idol. This is easier said than done. Many people tie their socioeconomic class to their identity. There is such a thing as your wealth (or lack of it) limiting your ability to connect with God. Where that line is, the Scripture is not clear, but we need to be aware that this is a possibility.

The message of Luke 12:13–21 is that money has no owners, only spenders. We should not define our identity by our wealth. The amount of money we gather does not determine the purpose and meaning of our lives. The tragedy of the rich man in Luke 12 is that he had no plans for his extra, other than to seek more. We must not allow wealth to lure us.

Acknowledgments

I want to extend my gratitude to the staff and ministry partners of World Impact. You bring out the best in me. Moreover, I thank my Lord and Savior, Jesus Christ. Without Him, none of this is possible!

About the Author

WHEN PEOPLE IN UNDER-RESOURCED COMMUNITIES experience trauma, the local church can be a beacon of hope. Alvin Sanders learned this from firsthand experience. While serving as an urban leader in the second most violent neighborhood in the country, a tragedy occurred. A police shooting with racial overtones rocked the neighborhood.

As a response, Alvin planted an innovative church that continues to care for, serve, and encourage people from all walks of life. Through this experience, he discovered his mission: to follow hard after God, love his family, and invest in those who invest in the poor.

Alvin is a churchman at heart. After church planting and pastoring, he served as a denominational leader with the Evangelical Free Church of America (EFCA) for seven years. While there, he directed the EFCA All People Initiative. His passion for church leaders made his move to World Impact in 2015 a natural fit. In November 2017, Alvin was named the president and CEO of World Impact.

Alvin is the author of *Bridging the Diversity Gap, Uncommon Church, and Redemptive Poverty Work.* His educational background includes a BS in Biblical Studies from Cincinnati Christian University and an MA in Religion & Urban Ministry from Trinity Evangelical Divinity School.

He earned a PhD in Educational Leadership from Miami University. Since 2004, he has served as an adjunct professor at various seminaries across the nation. Alvin is an avid reader in his free time and loves to follow his favorite sports teams. He is grateful for his amazing wife, Caroline, who maintains a counseling practice in their hometown of Cincinnati. They have been blessed with two wonderful daughters.

Further Your Redemptive Poverty Work Training

World Impact has a vision to see a healthy church in every community experiencing poverty. As a Christian leader, whether pastoral or lay leader, you, too, are called to this mission.

If you are looking to apply the Redemptive Poverty Work practices day to day in service to your neighbor, learn more about how you can apply these biblically based resources and expand God's kingdom right in your community.

Learn more: worldimpact.org/resources

World Impact Training Opportunities

Trauma Healing Training

Our mission is to see healthier churches in communities experiencing poverty. Trauma Healing supports this mission by restoring broken hearts, equipping and empowering leaders, partnering with local churches, and creating resilient, Christ-centered communities. Because when churches embrace trauma healing, they become powerful agents of transformation, strengthening both the church and the broader community.

Cornerstone Curriculum

Discover a high-quality training for Christian leaders who may not need or have the time for training that takes several years. It provides knowledge and skills for Christian leadership in a succinct format.

Urban Church Planting School

Whether you are planting a new church, preparing to replant (restart, revitalize, or relaunch) an existing church, seeking a proven process for transitioning to the next generation of pastoral leadership, or seeking to catalyze a church planting movement, there's a place for you and your team.

Capstone Curriculum

A seminary-level training program designed to equip learners with the knowledge and skills necessary for effective urban ministry and church leadership.

Prison Ministry

Our Prison Ministry empowers incarcerated men and women with training in evangelism, discipleship, and church planting so they can become powerful agents of change, transforming lives and advancing God's kingdom from within and as returning citizens.

Books for Further Reading

Church Plant Manual

by Rev. Ted Smith

Written for the urban context, World Impact's *Church Plant Manual* is a solid guidebook for teams to leverage.

This principle-based resource is designed to assist church plant teams to develop a strategic plan for their specific context and needs, whether they are planting a new church, preparing to replant (restart, revitalize, or relaunch) an existing church, seeking a process for transitioning to the next generation of pastoral leadership, or creating a church planting movement.

Fight the Good Fight of Faith: Playing Your Part in God's Unfolding Drama

by Rev. Don Allsman and Dr. Don L. Davis

Need discipleship curriculum for the urban context?

This practical, helpful resource is especially designed to help new and growing Christians become effective disciples and warriors for Christ. It is built entirely on the story of God as told in the Scriptures.

Uncommon Church: Community Transformation for the Common Good

by Rev. Dr. Alvin Sanders

How can the people of God develop churches in ways that help and do not hurt poor neighborhoods?

The local, urban church is the key to community transformation and plays three crucial roles of empowering, partnering, and reaching. Pastors and church planters interested in Christian community development in the context of urban neighborhoods will find practical insights into the power of the local church in this book.

Learn more about World Impact, how to support the mission, and other affordable and accessible training opportunities at worldimpact.org.

www.ingramcontent.com/pod-product-compliance
Lightning Source LLC
LaVergne TN
LVHW010624100826
845148LV00014B/3099

* 9 7 8 1 6 2 9 3 2 4 6 9 2 *